The Newest Emeril Lagasse
French Doors
Air Fryer Oven Cookbook

Super Simple & Quick Dual Zone Air Fryer Oven Recipes | 2000 Days of
Home-Made Dishes | with a BONUS 30-Day Meal Plan

Laree Holmes

Table of Contents

Introduction

Welcome to the culinary journey that will transform your kitchen experience! In this Emeril Lagasse French Door Air Fryer Cookbook, we embark on a flavorful adventure where simplicity meets innovation. Whether you're a novice in the kitchen or a seasoned chef, get ready to discover the wonders of air frying–a revolutionary cooking technique that will redefine the way you enjoy your favorite meals.

In the hustle and bustle of today's fast-paced world, we often find ourselves searching for quick, convenient, and healthier meal options. That's where the air fryer steps in as your trusty kitchen companion. It's not just a kitchen appliance; it's a game-changer that allows you to indulge in the irresistible taste and texture of your beloved fried foods, all while significantly reducing the use of oil.

This cookbook is designed with simplicity in mind, ensuring that every recipe is easy to follow, even for those with minimal cooking experience. From crispy appetizers to succulent main courses and delectable desserts, this cookbook covers a wide range of dishes to satisfy every plate.

As you flip through these pages, you'll find a treasure trove of mouthwatering recipes that combine traditional flavors with the efficiency of air frying. Whether you're craving classic comfort foods, exploring international cuisines, or seeking healthier alternatives, we've got you covered. This appliance comes with amazing accessories and parts.

But it's not just about the recipes; it's about unlocking the full potential of your air fryer. We've included handy tips, tricks, and techniques to ensure that every dish turns out perfectly. You'll be amazed at how this compact appliance can produce dishes that are not only delicious but also guilt-free. Emeril Lagasse French Door Air Fryer comes with many accessories and buttons and all are user-friendly.

So, whether you're a busy professional, a parent juggling multiple tasks, or simply someone who loves good food without the fuss, let this Emeril Lagasse French Door Air Fryer Cookbook be your go-to guide for creating quick, easy, and tantalizing meals. Get ready to embark on a culinary adventure that will leave your taste buds dancing and your kitchen filled with the aroma of success! Let's get started!

Fundamentals of Emeril Lagasse French Door Air Fryer

What is Emeril Lagasse French Door Air Fryer?

The Emeril Lagasse French Door Air Fryer is a versatile kitchen appliance designed to make cooking a breeze. Whether you are a kitchen expert or a newbie, this QuickStart guide will help you get started on your culinary journey with this innovative air fryer. It saves your time and stress as well as improves the cooking. This appliance comes with many parts and accessories such as Drip Tray, Wire Rack, Baking Pan, Rotisserie Spit, Crisper Tray, Fetch Tool, Grill plate, and Grill Plate Handle. There are many benefits and features of this appliance.

Benefits of Using Emeril Lagasse French Door Air Fryer

User-Friendly:

Handling the French door air fryer is a piece of cake and the user interface is very intuitive. There is a preset button for most common cooking modes: for roasting a turkey or making pizza, to dehydrating meat and steaming vegetables. Intuitive controls and preset cooking programs streamline the cooking process, allowing for easy operation and delicious results every time.

Versatile:

With the French door air fryer, you can finally try out all the recipes you have been planning to try but never had time for it or felt it was too much of a border to attempt cooking with your clunky old oven. It is an excellent for trying out all types of recipes. Whether they involve frying, roasting, or slow cooking, the Emeril has got you covered. One of the standout features of air fryers is their versatility. Beyond traditional frying, these appliances can roast, bake, grill, and even reheat food, offering a wide range of cooking options in a single device. This versatility makes air fryers suitable for preparing a variety of dishes, from crispy fries to tender meats and even desserts.

Safety features:

Unlike other air fryers that are all noise and increase the room temperature, the Emeril Lagasse French door air fryer is quite the opposite. This appliance has many safety features. Air fryers prioritize safety with features such as automatic shut-off timers, cool-touch exteriors, and built-in overheating protection. These safety measures provide peace of mind to users, allowing them to cook with confidence knowing that their appliance is designed with their well-being in mind.

Easy to clean:

Unlike traditional deep fryers, air fryers require minimal cleanup thanks to their non-stick cooking baskets and dishwasher-safe components. The removable parts make it easy to clean grease and food residue, saving time and effort in the kitchen. This appliance has a body made of stainless steel, which is a relief when you have to clean it or remove crumbs from icky places.

Parts and Accessories

Main Unit:

Constructed entirely of durable stainless steel, this appliance boasts robustness. It can be effortlessly cleaned using a moist sponge or cloth paired with a gentle detergent, ensuring convenience. It's important to steer clear of harsh, abrasive cleaners to preserve its integrity. Remember, under no circumstances should this appliance be submerged in water or any other liquids.

Door Handles:

Ensure that the handle is always used and refrain from touching the door. Both doors will open when one is opened. Take caution as the door may become excessively hot during cooking, posing a risk of injury.

Glass Doors:

High-quality tempered glass, known for its robustness and durability, retains heat effectively while ensuring uniform distribution to the food. It is crucial never to cook with these doors open.

Led Display:

Employed for the selection, adjustment of programming, or monitoring of cooking programs.

Control Panel:

Contains the Control Buttons and Knobs

Control Knob:

Used to select the preset cooking settings

Drip Tray:

Position the Drip Tray at the base of the appliance, positioned just underneath the heating elements. Always ensure the Drip Tray is in place before using the appliance. When cooking substantial or moist foods, the Drip Tray may accumulate liquid. If the Drip Tray fills more than halfway, it should be emptied. To do so while cooking, wearing oven mitts cautiously open the door and gently remove the Drip Tray from the appliance, taking care to avoid contact with the heating elements. Empty the contents of the Drip Tray and then reinsert it into the appliance. Close the door to resume the cooking process.

Wire Rack:

Utilize for the toasting of breads, bagels, and pizzas, as well as for baking, grilling, and roasting. Quantities may differ. When using baking pans and dishes for baking or cooking, ensure they are placed on a rack. Never directly cook anything on the heating elements.

Baking Pan:

Employ for baking and reheating a variety of dishes. Utilize deeper oven-safe pans and dishes within the appliance.

Rotisserie Spit:

Used for cooking chickens and meat on a spit while rotating.

Crisper Tray:

Utilize air circulation for oil-free frying to evenly distribute hot air throughout the food.

Rotisserie Fetch Tool:

Utilize this tool for safely handling hot food on the Rotisserie Spit, ensuring protection against burns. Remember to use hand protection when removing hot items from the appliance.

Grill Plate:

Use for grilling steaks, burgers, veggies, and more.

Grill Plate Handle:

Secure the Crisper Tray or the Grill Plate onto the appliance for easy removal.

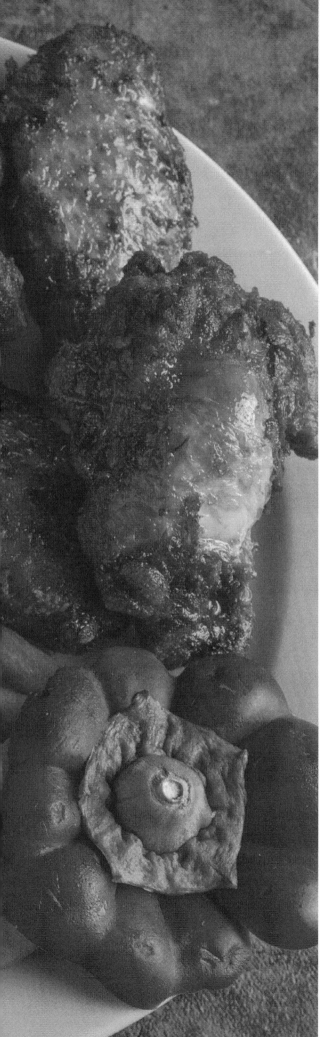

Here's how to use the accessories.

Wire Rack

Position the Drip Tray beneath the lowest heating elements located at the bottommost part of the appliance. Refer to the markings on the door to select the appropriate shelf position as per your recipe's requirements. Arrange your food on the Wire Rack and carefully slot it into the designated position.

Baking Pan

Position the Drip Tray beneath the lower heating elements located at the appliance's base. Refer to the markings on the door to select the appropriate cooking position as per your recipe. Arrange your food on the Baking Pan, and then slide the Baking Pan into the designated slot. Please be aware that the Baking Pan can also be placed on a shelf below the Crisper Tray or Wire Rack to capture any dripping from the food.

Crisper Tray

Position the Drip Tray beneath the lower heating elements situated at the base of the appliance. Utilize the guide markings on the door to select the recommended shelf level for your specific recipe. Arrange your food on the Crisper Tray and then place it into the designated slot. It's important to note that when preparing foods prone to dripping, like bacon or steak, it's advisable to employ the Baking Pan beneath the Tray or Rack to capture any juices and minimize smoke.

Grill Plate

Position the Drip Tray beneath the lower heating elements, situated at the appliance's lowest point. Arrange your food on the Grill Plate, and then slide it into shelf position 7.

Grill Plate Handle

Attach the larger connected hook of the Grill Plate Handle to the top part of the accessory, then gently pull the accessory out of the appliance until the larger hook is underneath it. Turn over the Grill Plate Handle and secure it to the accessory using the two smaller hooks. Carefully lift the accessory out of the appliance and place it on a heat-resistant surface. Note that the Grill Plate Handle can also be used to remove the Crisper Tray, but exercise caution as accessories will be hot. Avoid touching hot accessories with bare hands and always use a heat-resistant surface. Never carry the Crisper Tray or Grill Plate using the Grill Plate Handle; it is intended only for removing these accessories from the appliance.

Rotisserie Spit

Place the Drip Tray beneath the lower heating elements situated at the base of the appliance. Remove the Forks, and then thread the Rotisserie Spit lengthwise through the center of the food. Attach the Forks (A) onto each side of the Spit and fasten them securely using two Set Screws (B) It's advisable to insert the Rotisserie Forks into the food at varying angles to provide

better support. Hold the assembled Rotisserie Spit at a slight tilt, with the left side elevated higher than the right, and insert the right side of the Spit into the Rotisserie connection within the appliance. Once the right side is firmly in position, insert the left side of the Spit into the Rotisserie connection located on the left side of the appliance. And how about removing the rotisserie spit: Utilize the Fetch Tool to secure the lower ends of the shaft on both left and right sides of the Rotisserie Spit assembly. Gently shift the Rotisserie Spit towards the left to disengage it from the Rotisserie Socket. With caution, extract and detach the Rotisserie Spit from the appliance. To extract food from the Rotisserie Spit, rotate to loosen the screws on one of the Rotisserie Forks, and then repeat the process for the second fork. Slide the food off the Rotisserie Spit.

The Control Panel

Cooking Presets:

Utilize the Program Selection Knob to choose a cooking preset. Activate any button on the Control Panel or adjust the Program Selection Knob to illuminate the available cooking presets.

Fan Display:

Illuminates when the appliance's fan is on.

Heating Element Display:

Illuminates when the top and/or bottom heating elements are on.

Temperature Display:

Displays the current set cooking temperature.

Time Display:

During the preheating phase of the appliance, it will indicate "PH." Throughout the cooking cycle, it will show the remaining cooking duration.

Mute Display:

Illuminates when the Mute Function is activated.

Temperature Button:

You have the flexibility to modify preset temperatures with ease. Adjusting the temperature during the cooking process is simple: just press the Temperature Button and turn the dial to set the desired temperature. Additionally, you can switch between Fahrenheit and Celsius by pressing and holding the Temperature Button.

Fan Button:

Press the button to activate or deactivate the fan when paired with specific presets and to adjust the fan speed between high, low, or off settings. To modify the fan speed, ensure a cooking preset is initiated beforehand. Following the completion of a cooking cycle, hold down the Fan Button for 3 seconds to engage the appliance's manual cool-down feature.

Time Button:

You have the flexibility to override preset times. You can adjust the cooking time at any point during the cycle by pressing the Time Button and then turning the dial to your desired time setting.

Light Button:

You can choose to illuminate the appliance's interior at any point during the cooking process.

Mute Function:

When the Mute Function is activated, the Mute icon will light up, and audible signals linked to different programming functions, such as the alert signaling the conclusion of the cooking cycle, will be silenced. To toggle the Mute Function on or off, press and hold the Light Button for duration of 3 seconds.

Start/Pause Button:

Press to begin or pause the cooking process at any time.

Cancel Button:

You may select this button at any time to cancel the cooking process. Hold the Cancel Button for 3 seconds to power off the appliance).

Control Knob:

To navigate through preset modes, utilize the scrolling feature. The Control Knob's surrounding ring illuminates in blue upon powering up the appliance. Once a preset is chosen, the ring shifts to red, reverting to blue once the cooking cycle finishes.

The time and temperature on the chart below refer the basic default settings. As you become familiar with the appliance, you will be able to make minor adjustments to suit your taste. Note: The appliance has a memory feature that will keep your last program setting used. To reset this feature, unplug the appliance, wait 1 minute and power the appliance back on.

Preset Mode Chart:

Preset	Fan Speed	Halfway timer	Preheat	Default Temperature	Default Time
Air Fry	High	Y	N	400°F/205°C	15 mins.
Grill	Low/off	Y	Y	450°F/230°C	15 mins.
Defrost	Low/off	Y	N	180°F/80°C	20 mins.
Bake	High/low/off	Y	Y	350°F/175°C	25 mins.
Rotisserie	High	N	N	375°F/190°C	40 mins.
Toast	N/A	N	N	4 Slices	6 mins.
Broil	High	Y	Y	400°F/205°C	10 mins.
Slow Cook	High/Low/off	N	N	225°F/105°C	4 hrs.
Roast	High/Low/off	Y	Y	350°F/175°C	35 mins.
Dehydrate	Low	N	N	120°F/50°C	12 hrs
Reheat	High/Low/off	Y	N	280°F/135°C	20 mins.
Warm	Low/off	N	N	160°F/70°C	1 hr

Preheating:

Certain presets come with a preheating feature. Upon choosing a preset equipped with this function, the control panel will indicate "PH" instead of the cooking duration until the appliance attains the designated temperature. Following this, the cooking timer will initiate its countdown. In certain recipes, it is advisable to introduce food to

the appliance post-preheating. Given that the appliance will be hot, exercise caution and utilize oven mitts when placing food inside.

Halfway Timer:

This appliance offers various presets, including a convenient halfway timer. This timer alerts you when the cooking process has reached its midpoint, allowing you to take action for more even cooking. For food in the Crisper Tray, carefully use oven mitts to shake it. When flipping items like burgers or steak, employ tongs for a safe maneuver. To ensure proper rotation of accessories, switch their positions within the appliance. For instance, if the Crisper Tray is on shelf position 2 and the Wire Rack is on shelf position 6, swap them so that the Crisper Tray moves to shelf position 6 and the Wire Rack to shelf position 2.

Dual Fan Speeds:

When utilizing certain presets on this appliance, you have the option to adjust the speed of the top-mounted fan. Operating the fan at a high speed facilitates the circulation of superheated air around your food during cooking, ensuring even cooking for a variety of dishes. Conversely, opting for a lower fan speed is recommended for delicate foods like baked goods. The "Preset Chart" section provides a breakdown of available fan settings for each preset, with the default fan speed highlighted in bold for quick reference.

Manual Cool-Down Function:

Once a cooking cycle concludes, you have the option to activate the appliance's manual cool-down function by pressing and holding the Fan Button for 3 seconds. This initiates a process where the top fan runs for 3 minutes, effectively cooling down the appliance. It's particularly useful for lowering the interior temperature after cooking at a lower heat setting than the previous cycle. During this manual cool-down phase, several indicators signal its operation: the light around the Fan Display icon illuminates, the Program Selection Knob turns red, and the Cooking Presets section of the Control Panel dims. If desired, you can adjust the fan speed from high to low by pressing the Fan Button while the manual cool-down function is active. Pressing the Fan Button again cancels the manual cool-down process. It's important to note that while the manual cool-down function is in progress, the Program Selection Knob is inactive for choosing cooking presets. However, you can terminate the manual cool-down function at any point by pressing the Cancel Button.

Before the First Use

- Familiarize yourself with all included documents, cautionary stickers, and product labels.
- Carefully eliminate any packaging materials, labels, or stickers from the cooking appliance.
- Thoroughly cleanse all components and accessories used during the cooking process using warm, soapy water, with handwashing being the preferred method.
- Avoid immersing or washing the cooking appliance in water; instead, utilize a clean, damp cloth to wipe both the interior and exterior surfaces.
- Prior to cooking, preheat the appliance for several minutes to allow any residual protective coating to dissipate. Following this initial heating process, cleanse the appliance with warm, soapy water and a dishcloth.

Step-By-Step Using it

- Position the appliance on a steady, even surface that can withstand heat. Ensure that the appliance is used in an area with good air circulation and away from hot surfaces, other objects or appliances and any combustible materials.
- Ensure that the appliance is plugged into a dedicated power outlet.
- Select the cooking accessory for your recipe.
- Place food to be cooked in appliance and close the doors.
- Select a preset mode by using the Control Knob to scroll though the presets and pressing the Start/ Pause Button to select the preset. The cooking cycle will begin. Note that some cooking presets include a preheating feature.
- After the cooking cycle has started, you can adjust the cooking temperature by pressing the Temperature Button and then using the Control Knob to adjust the temperature. You can also adjust the cooking time by pressing the Time Button and using the Control Knob to adjust the cooking time. NOTE: When toasting bread or a bagel, you control the lightness or darkness by adjusting the same knobs. When the cooking process is complete and the cooking time has elapsed, the appliance will beep several times. Leaving the appliance idle (untouched) for 3 minutes will automatically turn the appliance off.

Tips

- Smaller foods generally need less cooking time compared to larger ones.
- Larger portions or quantities may necessitate extended cooking periods.
- For a crisper texture, lightly mist fresh potatoes with vegetable oil just before cooking.
- Snacks typically baked in an oven can also be prepared using this appliance.

- Utilize premade dough for quick and convenient filled snacks, as it requires less cooking time than homemade dough.
- When baking foods like cakes or quiches, place a baking pan or oven dish on the wire rack inside the appliance. Using a tin or dish is advisable for delicate or filled foods.
- DO NOT use this appliance for anything other than its intended use.
- DO NOT use the appliance outdoors.
- ALWAYS unplug the appliance after use.
- DO NOT clean with metal scouring pads. Pieces can break off the pad and touch electrical parts, creating a risk of electric shock. Use non-metallic scrub pads.
- DO NOT store any materials, other than manufacturer recommended accessories, in this appliance when not in use.
- DO NOT place your appliance on a cooktop, even if the cooktop is cool, because you could accidentally turn the cooktop on, causing a fire, damaging the appliance, your cooktop, and your home.
- DO NOT cover the Drip Tray or any part of the appliance with metal foil. This will cause overheating of the appliance. To disconnect, turn the control to off and then remove the plug from the wall outlet. To turn off the appliance, press the Cancel Button. The indicator light around the Control Knob will change color from red to blue and then the appliance will turn off.

Cleaning and Storage

Cleaning:

Ensure the appliance is cleaned after each use. First, disconnect the power cord from the wall socket and wait until the appliance has cooled completely.

Then, follow these steps:

- Gently wipe the exterior of the appliance using a warm, damp cloth and a mild detergent.
- Clean the appliance doors by softly scrubbing both sides with warm, soapy water and a damp cloth. Avoid soaking or submerging the appliance in water or using a dishwasher.
- For the interior, use hot water, mild detergent, and a nonabrasive sponge to clean. Avoid scrubbing the heating coils to prevent damage. Rinse the appliance thoroughly with a clean, damp cloth and ensure no standing water remains inside.
- Use a nonabrasive cleaning brush to remove any

stubborn food residue if necessary.
* Soak accessories with caked-on food in warm, soapy water for easy removal. Hand-washing is recommended.

Storage:

* Disconnect the appliance from power and allow it to cool down completely.
* Ensure that all parts are free from dirt and moisture.
* Position the appliance in a spot that is both clean and dry.

Troubleshooting

Problem: 1

The appliance does not work.

Possible Cause:
1. The appliance is not plugged in.
2. You have not turned the appliance on by setting the preparation time and temperature.
3. The appliance is not plugged into a dedicated power outlet

Solution:
1. Plug power cord into wall socket.
2. Set the temperature and time.
3. Plug the appliance into a dedicated power outlet.

Problem: 2

Food is not cooked.

Possible Cause:
1. The appliance is overloaded.
2. The temperature is set too low

Solution:
1. Use smaller batches for more even cooking.
2. Raise temperature and continue cooking.

Problem: 3

White smoke comes from appliance.

Possible Cause:
1. Oil is being used.
2. Accessories have excess grease residue from previous cooking.

Solution:
1. Wipe down to remove excess oil.
2. Clean the components and appliance interior after each use.

Problem: 4

Food is not fried evenly.

Possible Cause:
1. Some foods need to be turned during the cooking process.
2. Foods of different sizes are being cooked together.
3. Accessories need to be rotated, especially if food is being cooked on multiple accessories simultaneously.

Solution:
1. Check halfway through process and turn food if needed.
2. Cook similar-sized foods together.
3. Rotate the accessories halfway through the cooking time.

Frequently Asked Questions

1. Does the appliance need time to heat up?
The device boasts an intelligent function that automatically heats up to the designated temperature prior to initiating the countdown timer. This functionality applies to all preset modes except for Toast, Bagel, and Dehydrate.

2. Is it possible to stop the cooking cycle at any time?
You can use the Cancel Button to stop the cooking cycle.

3. Can I check the food during the cooking process?
You can check the cooking process by pressing the Light Button or pressing the Start/Pause Button and then opening the door.

4-Week Meal Plan

Week 1

Day 1:
Breakfast: Delicious Jalapeño and Bacon Breakfast Pizza
Lunch: Zucchini and Spinach Stuffed Portobellos
Snack: Crispy Avocado Fries
Dinner: Gingered Turmeric Chicken Thighs
Dessert: Almond Butter Chocolate Chip Balls

Day 2:
Breakfast: Sausage Egg Cups
Lunch: Zucchini-Mushroom Burgers
Snack: Pork Sausage-Stuffed Mushrooms
Dinner: Hearty Bacon and Blue Cheese Burgers
Dessert: Crispy Cinnamon Pork Rinds

Day 3:
Breakfast: Simple Mini Bagels
Lunch: Crispy Bacon-Wrapped Asparagus
Snack: Hot & Spicy Turkey Meatballs
Dinner: Cajun Parmesan Lobster Tails
Dessert: Refreshing Lime Bars

Day 4:
Breakfast: Savory Pizza Eggs
Lunch: Italian Burrata-Stuffed Tomatoes
Snack: Crispy Parmesan Zucchini Fries
Dinner: Traditional Hasselback Alfredo Chicken
Dessert: Pecan and Chocolate Chip Brownies

Day 5:
Breakfast: Cheese Jalapeño Egg Cups
Lunch: Cheese Broccoli Sticks with Ranch Dressing
Snack: Salami Cream Cheese Roll-Ups
Dinner: Traditional Mini Meatloaf
Dessert: Tasty Mini Cheesecake

Day 6:
Breakfast: Crunchy Chocolate and Nuts Granola
Lunch: Roasted Brussels Sprouts
Snack: Fried Ranch Parmesan Pickles
Dinner: Classic Shrimp Scampi
Dessert: Chocolate Chip Pan Cookie

Day 7:
Breakfast: Bacon-Wrapped Egg Avocado
Lunch: Perfect Zucchini Noodles
Snack: Crunchy Bacon-Wrapped Mozzarella Sticks
Dinner: Perfect Chicken Pesto Pizzas
Dessert: Lemony Blackberry Crisp

Week 2

Day 1:
Breakfast: Crispy Double-Dipped Mini Cinnamon Biscuits
Lunch: Best Cheesy Baked Asparagus
Snack: Tasty Buffalo Cauliflower Bites
Dinner: Savory Garlic Parmesan Drumsticks
Dessert: Yummy Halle Berries-and-Cream Cobbler

Day 2:
Breakfast: Simple Meritage Eggs
Lunch: Jalapeño and Cheese Cauliflower Mash
Snack: Crispy Ranch Kale Chips
Dinner: Quick Pigs in a Blanket
Dessert: Mini Chocolate Espresso Cheesecake

Day 3:
Breakfast: Bell Pepper and Ham Egg Cups
Lunch: Tasty Garlic Parmesan–Roasted Cauliflower
Snack: Hot Cauliflower with Blue Cheese Dressing
Dinner: Crunchy Pecan-Crusted Catfish
Dessert: Crispy Pecan Snowball Cookies

Day 4:
Breakfast: Bacon-Wrapped Egg Avocado
Lunch: Dijon Roasted Cabbage
Snack: Spicy Nacho Avocado Fries
Dinner: Italian Chicken Parmesan
Dessert: Homemade Chocolate Doughnut Holes

Day 5:
Breakfast: Pepperoni Breakfast Pizza
Lunch: Cheesy Cauliflower Rice Balls
Snack: Delicious Bourbon Chicken Wings
Dinner: Tasty Salisbury Steak with Mushroom Onion Gravy
Dessert: Delicious Chocolate Soufflés

Day 6:
Breakfast: Classic Denver Omelet
Lunch: Cheese Roasted Broccoli
Snack: Crispy Bacon-Wrapped Pickle Poppers
Dinner: Homemade Coconut Shrimp with Spicy Mayo
Dessert: Fluffy Little French Fudge Cakes

Day 7:
Breakfast: Breakfast Biscuit Sammies
Lunch: Flavorful Buttery Mushrooms
Snack: Doro Wat Chicken Wings
Dinner: Delicious Chicken Pesto Parmigiana
Dessert: Easy Chilled Strawberry Pie

Week 3

Day 1:
Breakfast: Low-Carb Chocolate Chip Muffins
Lunch: Low-Carb Sweet Pepper Nachos
Snack: Vegan Broccoli and Carrot Bites
Dinner: Mayo Broccoli and Cheese Stuffed Chicken
Dessert: Crispy Brown Sugar Cookies

Day 2:
Breakfast: Cheesy Bacon and Egg Calzones
Lunch: Spinach Artichoke–Stuffed Peppers
Snack: Cheesy Bacon-Wrapped Jalapeño Poppers
Dinner: Lamb Koftas with Cucumber-Yogurt Dip
Dessert: Pumpkin Spiced Pork Rinds

Day 3:
Breakfast: Classic Denver Eggs
Lunch: Fresh Pesto Vegetable Skewers
Snack: Vinegary Pork Belly Chips
Dinner: Everything Bagel Ahi Tuna Steaks
Dessert: Mini Flourless Chocolate Cakes

Day 4:
Breakfast: Homemade Cinnamon Rolls
Lunch: Crispy Cheese Eggplant Rounds
Snack: Cheese-Stuffed Mushrooms
Dinner: Crispy Pickle-Brined Fried Chicken
Dessert: Protein Doughnut Holes

Day 5:
Breakfast: Cheesy Egg Stuffed Bell Pepper
Lunch: Roasted Cabbage Steaks
Snack: Easy Pepperoni Chips
Dinner: Perfect Marinated Rib Eye
Dessert: Low-Carb Chocolate-Covered Maple Bacon

Day 6:
Breakfast: Light Egg White Cups
Lunch: Delicious Eggplant Parmesan
Snack: Crispy Bacon-Wrapped Onion Rings
Dinner: Easy Bacon-Wrapped Scallops
Dessert: Pumpkin Roasted Spice Pecans

Day 7:
Breakfast: Crunchy Cinnamon Granola
Lunch: Cheesy Zucchini Fritters
Snack: Basic Three Cheese Dip
Dinner: Simple Buttery Pork Chops
Dessert: Simple Toasted Coconut Flakes

Week 4

Day 1:
Breakfast: Fresh Blueberry Muffins
Lunch: Butter Roasted Spaghetti Squash
Snack: Tasty Mini Greek Meatballs
Dinner: Simple Pecan-Crusted Chicken Tenders
Dessert: Homemade Lemon Poppy Seed Macaroons

Day 2:
Breakfast: Traditional Scotch Eggs
Lunch: White Cheddar Mushroom Soufflés
Snack: Chewy Sweet-Spicy Beef Jerky
Dinner: Greek Stuffed Beef Tenderloin
Dessert: Baked Chocolate Meringue Cookies

Day 3:
Breakfast: Nutritious Veggie Frittata
Lunch: Homemade Alfredo Eggplant Stacks
Snack: Homemade Cauliflower Buns
Dinner: Mayo Crab-Stuffed Avocado Boats
Dessert: Mini Peanut Butter Cheesecake

Day 4:
Breakfast: Super-Easy Bacon Strips
Lunch: Roasted Cauliflower
Snack: Cheesy Pepperoni Rolls
Dinner: Creamy Chicken Cordon Bleu Casserole
Dessert: Perfect Lemon Curd Pavlova

Day 5:
Breakfast: Breakfast Lamb Patties with Tzatziki Sauce
Lunch: Lime Gingered Cauliflower Rice
Snack: Creamy Buffalo Chicken Dip
Dinner: Old Bay Crab Cakes
Dessert: Refreshing Lime Bars

Day 6:
Breakfast: Quick Bacon-Wrapped Hot Dog
Lunch: Air Fryer Garlic Thyme Mushrooms
Snack: Flavorful Ranch Chicken Bites
Dinner: Tender Reverse Seared Ribeye
Dessert: Sweet Peanut Butter Cookies

Day 7:
Breakfast: Easy Spiced Muffins
Lunch: Spinach Artichoke Cheese Tart
Snack: Corned Beef Prosciutto Rolls
Dinner: Pistachio-Crusted Rack of Lamb
Dessert: Basic Olive Oil Cake

Chapter 1 Breakfast

Traditional Scotch Eggs

Prep Time: 10 minutes | Cook Time: 12 minutes | Serves: 8

1 large egg, whisked	½ teaspoon salt
1 pound ground pork breakfast sausage	¼ teaspoon ground black pepper
½ cup blanched finely ground almond flour	8 large hard-boiled eggs, shells removed

1. In a large bowl, mix raw egg with sausage, salt, flour, and pepper. 2. Form ¼ cup of the mixture around 1 hard-boiled egg, completely covering the egg. Repeat with remaining mixture and hard-boiled eggs. 3. Place eggs on the Crisper Tray and slide the Tray into shelf position 4/5. Select the Egg setting. Set the cooking temperature to 400°F/204°C and the cooking time to 12 minutes. Turn halfway through cooking. 4. Eggs will be done when browned. Let eggs cool 5 minutes before serving.

Crunchy Cinnamon Granola

Prep Time: 10 minutes | Cook Time: 7 minutes | Serves: 4

2 cups shelled pecans, chopped	2 tablespoons granular erythritol
1 cup unsweetened coconut flakes	1 teaspoon ground cinnamon
1 cup slivered almonds	

1. In a large bowl, mix up all ingredients. Place mixture into an ungreased 6" round nonstick baking dish that fits in the appliance. 2. Slide the Crisper Tray with the dish on top into shelf position 4/5. Select the Air Fry setting. Set the cooking temperature to 320°F/160°C and the cooking time to 7 minutes. Stir halfway through cooking. 3. Let cool in dish 10 minutes before serving. Store in airtight container at room temperature up to 5 days.

Nutritious Veggie Frittata

Prep Time: 15 minutes | Cook Time: 12 minutes | Serves: 4

6 large eggs	¼ cup chopped yellow onion
¼ cup heavy whipping cream	¼ cup chopped green bell pepper
½ cup chopped broccoli	

1. In a large bowl, beat eggs and heavy whipping cream. Mix in onion, broccoli, and bell pepper. 2. Pour into a 6" round oven-safe baking dish that fits in the appliance. Slide the Crisper Tray with the dish on top into shelf position 4/5. 3. Select the Air Fry setting. Set the cooking temperature to 350°F/176°C and the cooking time to 12 minutes. 4. Eggs should be firm and cooked fully when the frittata is done. Serve warm.

Perfect Pumpkin Spice Muffins

Prep Time: 10 minutes | Cook Time: 15 minutes | Serves: 6

1 cup blanched finely ground almond flour	½ teaspoon ground cinnamon
½ cup granular erythritol	¼ teaspoon ground nutmeg
½ teaspoon baking powder	1 teaspoon vanilla extract
¼ cup unsalted butter, softened	2 large eggs
¼ cup pure pumpkin purée	

1. In a large bowl, mix erythritol, baking powder, butter, pumpkin purée, almond flour, cinnamon, nutmeg, and vanilla. 2. Gently stir in eggs. 3. Evenly pour the batter into six silicone muffin cups. Place muffin cups on the Crisper Tray and slide the Tray into shelf position 4/5, working in batches if necessary. 4. Select the Air Fry setting. Set the cooking temperature to 300°F/148°C and the cooking time to 15 minutes. 5. When completely cooked, a toothpick inserted in center will come out mostly clean. Serve warm.

Breakfast Lamb Patties with Tzatziki Sauce

Prep Time: 10 minutes | Cook Time: 40 minutes | Serves: 8

Patties:

2 pounds ground lamb or beef
½ cup diced red onions
¼ cup sliced black olives
2 tablespoons tomato sauce

1 teaspoon dried oregano leaves
1 teaspoon Greek seasoning
2 cloves garlic, minced
1 teaspoon fine sea salt

Tzatziki:

1 cup full-fat sour cream
1 small cucumber, chopped
½ teaspoon fine sea salt

½ teaspoon garlic powder, or 1 minced garlic clove
¼ teaspoon dried dill weed, or 1 teaspoon finely chopped fresh dill

For Garnish/Serving:

½ cup crumbled feta cheese (about 2 ounces)
Diced red onions

Sliced black olives
Sliced cucumbers

1. Place the ground lamb, onions, olives, tomato sauce, oregano, Greek seasoning, garlic, and salt in a large bowl. Mix well to combine the ingredients. 2. Using your hands, form the mixture into sixteen 3-inch patties. Place about 8 of the patties in the Crisper Tray. Slide the Crisper Tray into shelf position 4/5. Select the Air Fry setting. Set the cooking temperature to 350°F and the cooking time to 20 minutes. Press Start/Pause to begin cooking. Flip them halfway through the cooking time. 3. Remove the patties and place them on a serving platter. Repeat with the remaining patties. 4. While the patties cook, make the tzatziki: Place all the ingredients in a small bowl and stir well. Cover and store in the fridge until ready to serve. Garnish with ground black pepper before serving. 5. Serve the patties with a dollop of tzatziki, a sprinkle of crumbled feta cheese, diced red onions, sliced black olives, and sliced cucumbers. 6. Store leftovers in an airtight container in the refrigerator for up to 5 days or in the freezer for up to a month. Reheat the patties in a preheated 390°F air fryer for a few minutes, until warmed through.

Spicy Cheese Quiche

Prep Time: 10 minutes | Cook Time: 1 hour | Serves: 8

Crust:

1¼ cups blanched almond flour
1¼ cups grated Parmesan or Gouda cheese (about 3¾ ounces)

¼ teaspoon fine sea salt
1 large egg, beaten

Filling:

½ cup chicken or beef broth (or vegetable broth for vegetarian)
1 cup shredded Swiss cheese (about 4 ounces)
4 ounces cream cheese (½ cup)
1 tablespoon unsalted butter, melted
4 large eggs, beaten

⅓ cup minced leeks or sliced green onions
¾ teaspoon fine sea salt
⅛ teaspoon cayenne pepper
Chopped green onions, for garnish

1. Grease a 6-inch pie pan. Spray two large pieces of parchment paper with avocado oil and set them on the countertop. 2. Make the crust: In a medium bowl, combine the flour, cheese, and salt and mix well. Add the egg and mix until the dough is well combined and stiff. 3. Place the dough in the center of one of the greased pieces of parchment. Top with the other piece of parchment. Using a rolling pin, roll out the dough into a circle about 1/16 inch thick. 4. Press the pie crust into the prepared pie pan. Slide the wire rack into shelf position 4/5. Place the pie pan on the wire rack. Select the Bake. Set the temperature to 325°F and the time to 12 minutes. Press Start/Pause to begin cooking. Cook until it starts to lightly brown. 5. While the crust bakes, make the filling: In a large bowl, combine the broth, Swiss cheese, cream cheese, and butter. Stir in the eggs, leeks, salt, and cayenne pepper. When the crust is ready, pour the mixture into the crust. 6. Place the quiche in the air fryer and bake for 15 minutes. Turn the heat down to 300°F and bake for an additional 30 minutes, or until a knife inserted 1 inch from the edge comes out clean. You may have to cover the edges of the crust with foil to prevent burning. 7. Allow the quiche to cool for 10 minutes before garnishing it with chopped green onions and cutting it into wedges. 8. Store leftovers in an airtight container in the refrigerator for up to 4 days or in the freezer for up to a month. Reheat in a preheated 350°F air fryer for a few minutes, until warmed through.

Easy Shakshuka

Prep Time: 5 minutes | Cook Time: 6 minutes | Serves: 1

½ cup salsa
2 large eggs, room temperature
½ teaspoon fine sea salt
For Garnish:
2 tablespoons cilantro leaves

¼ teaspoon smoked paprika
⅛ teaspoon ground cumin

1. Place the salsa in a casserole dish that will fit into your air fryer. Crack the eggs into the salsa and sprinkle them with the salt, paprika, and cumin. 2. Slide the Wire Rack into shelf position 6. Place the casserole dish on the Wire Rack. Select the Bake setting. Set the cooking temperature to 400°F and the cooking time to 6 minutes. Press Start/Pause to begin cooking. Cook until the egg whites are set and the yolks are cooked to your liking. 3. Remove from the air fryer and garnish with the cilantro before serving. 4. Best served fresh.

Avocado Egg Boats

Prep Time: 5 minutes | Cook Time: 10 minutes | Serves: 2

1 large Hass avocado, halved and pitted
2 thin slices ham
2 large eggs
2 tablespoons green onions, chopped, plus more for garnish

½ teaspoon fine sea salt
¼ teaspoon ground black pepper
¼ cup shredded cheddar cheese (omit for dairy-free)

1. Place a slice of ham into the cavity of each avocado half. Crack an egg on top of the ham, then sprinkle on the green onions, salt, and pepper. 2. Place the avocado halves in the Crisper Tray. Slide the Crisper Tray into shelf position 4/5. Select the Air Fry setting. Set the cooking temperature to 400°F and the cooking time to 10 minutes. Press Start/Pause to begin cooking. Cook until the egg is cooked to your desired doneness. Top with the cheese (if using) and cook for 30 seconds more, or until the cheese is melted. Garnish with chopped green onions. 3. Best served fresh. Store extras in an airtight container in the fridge for up to 4 days. 4. Reheat in a preheated 350°F air fryer for a few minutes, until warmed through.

Homemade Everything Bagels

Prep Time: 15 minutes | Cook Time: 14 minutes | Serves: 6

1¾ cups shredded mozzarella cheese or goat cheese mozzarella
2 tablespoons unsalted butter or coconut oil
1 large egg, beaten
1 tablespoon apple cider vinegar

1 cup blanched almond flour
1 tablespoon baking powder
⅛ teaspoon fine sea salt
1½ teaspoons everything bagel seasoning

1. Make the dough: Put the mozzarella and butter in a large microwave-safe bowl and microwave for 1 to 2 minutes, until the cheese is entirely melted. Stir well. Add the egg and vinegar. Using a hand mixer on medium, combine well. Add the almond flour, baking powder, and salt and, using the mixer, combine well. 2. Lay a piece of parchment paper on the countertop and place the dough on it. Knead it for about 3 minutes. The dough should be a little sticky but pliable. (If the dough is too sticky, chill it in the refrigerator for an hour or overnight.) 3. Spray the Baking Pan with avocado oil. 4. Divide the dough into 6 equal portions. Roll 1 portion into a log that is 6 inches long and about ½ inch thick. Form the log into a circle and seal the edges together, making a bagel shape. Repeat with the remaining portions of dough, making 6 bagels. 5. Place the bagels on the greased baking pan. Spray the bagels with avocado oil and top with everything bagel seasoning, pressing the seasoning into the dough with your hands. 6. Slide the Baking Pan into shelf position 4/5. Select the Bake setting. Set the cooking temperature to 350°F and the cooking time to 14 minutes. Press Start/Pause to begin cooking. Cook until cooked through and golden brown, flipping after 6 minutes. 7. Remove the bagels from the air fryer and let them cool slightly before slicing them in half and serving. Store leftovers in an airtight container in the fridge for up to 4 days or in the freezer for up to a month.

Keto Cream Cheese Danish

Prep Time: 15 minutes | Cook Time: 20 minutes | Serves: 6

Pastry:

3 large eggs

¼ teaspoon cream of tartar

¼ cup vanilla-flavored egg white protein powder

¼ cup Swerve confectioners'-style sweetener or equivalent amount of liquid or powdered sweetener, or 1 teaspoon stevia glycerite

3 tablespoons full-fat sour cream (or coconut cream for dairy-free)

1 teaspoon vanilla extract

Filling:

4 ounces cream cheese (½ cup) (or Kite Hill brand cream cheese style spread for dairy-free), softened

2 large egg yolks (from above)

¼ cup Swerve confectioners'-style sweetener or equivalent amount of liquid or powdered sweetener, or ½ teaspoon stevia glycerite

1 teaspoon vanilla extract

¼ teaspoon ground cinnamon

Drizzle:

1-ounce cream cheese (2 tablespoons) (or Kite Hill brand cream cheese style spread for dairy-free), softened

1 tablespoon Swerve confectioners'-style sweetener or equivalent amount of liquid or powdered sweetener, or 1 drop stevia glycerite

1 tablespoon unsweetened, unflavored almond milk (or heavy cream for nut-free)

1. Spray a casserole dish that will fit in your air fryer with avocado oil. 2. Make the pastry: Separate the eggs, putting all the whites in a large bowl, one yolk in a medium-sized bowl, and two yolks in a small bowl. Beat all the egg yolks and set aside. 3. Add the cream of tartar to the egg whites. Whip the whites with a hand mixer until very stiff, then turn the hand mixer's setting to low and slowly add the protein powder while mixing. Mix until only just combined; if you mix too long, the whites will fall. Set aside. 4. To the egg yolk in the medium-sized bowl, add the sweetener, sour cream, and vanilla extract. Mix well. Slowly pour the yolk mixture into the egg whites and gently combine. Dollop 6 equal-sized mounds of batter into the casserole dish. Use the back of a large spoon to make an indentation on the top of each mound. Set aside. 5. Make the filling: Place the cream cheese in a small bowl and stir to break it up. Add the 2 remaining egg yolks, the sweetener, cinnamon and vanilla extract and stir until well combined. Divide the filling among the mounds of batter, pouring it into the indentations on the tops. 6. Slide the Wire Rack into shelf position 6. Place the casserole dish on the Wire Rack. Select the Bake setting. Set the cooking temperature to 300°F and the cooking time to 20 minutes. Press Start/Pause to begin cooking. Bake until golden brown. 7. While the Danish bake, make the drizzle: In a small bowl, stir the cream cheese to break it up. Stir in the sweetener and almond milk. Place the mixture in a piping bag or a small resealable plastic bag with one corner snipped off. After the Danish have cooled, pipe the drizzle over the Danish. 8. Store leftovers in airtight container in the fridge for up to 4 days.

Perfect Pavlova

Prep Time: 15 minutes | Cook Time: 1 hour | Serves: 4

3 large egg whites

¼ teaspoon cream of tartar

¾ cup Swerve confectioners'-style sweetener or equivalent amount of powdered sweetener

1 teaspoon ground cinnamon

1 teaspoon maple extract

Toppings:

½ cup heavy cream

3 tablespoons Swerve confectioners'-style sweetener or equivalent amount of powdered sweetener, plus more for garnish

Fresh strawberries (optional)

1. Thoroughly grease a 7-inch pie pan with butter or coconut oil. Place a large bowl in the refrigerator to chill. 2. In a small bowl, combine the egg whites and cream of tartar. Using a hand mixer, beat until soft peaks form. Turn the mixer to low and slowly sprinkle in the sweetener while mixing until completely incorporated. Add the cinnamon and maple extract and beat on medium-high until the peaks become stiff. 3. Spoon the mixture into the greased pie pan, then smooth it across the bottom, up the sides, and onto the rim of the pie pan to form a shell. Slide the wire rack into shelf position 4/5. Place the pie pan on the wire rack. Select the Bake. Set the temperature to 275°F and the time to 45 minutes. Press Start/Pause to begin cooking. 4. When cooking time is up, cook for 15 minutes more. Then turn off the air fryer and let the shell stand in the air fryer for another 20 minutes. Once the shell has set, transfer it to the refrigerator to chill for 20 minutes or the freezer to chill for 10 minutes. 5. While the shell sets and chills, make the topping: Remove the large bowl from the refrigerator and place the heavy cream in it. Whip with a hand mixer on high until soft peaks form. Add the sweetener and beat until medium peaks form. Taste and adjust the sweetness to your liking. 6. Place the chilled shell on a serving platter and spoon on the cream topping. Top with the strawberries, if desired, and garnish with powdered sweetener. Slice and serve. 7. If you won't be eating the pavlova right away, store the shell and topping in separate airtight containers in the refrigerator for up to 3 days.

Breakfast Pork Sausage Cobbler

Prep Time: 20 minutes | Cook Time: 30 minutes | Serves: 4

Filling:

10 ounces bulk pork sausage, crumbled	½ teaspoon ground black pepper
¼ cup minced onions	1 (8-ounce) package cream cheese (or Kite Hill brand cream cheese style spread for dairy-free), softened
2 cloves garlic, minced	
½ teaspoon fine sea salt	¾ cup beef or chicken broth

Biscuits:

3 large egg whites	¼ teaspoon fine sea salt
¾ cup blanched almond flour	2½ tablespoons very cold unsalted butter, cut into ¼-inch pieces
1 teaspoon baking powder	Fresh thyme leaves, for garnish

1. Place the sausage, onions, and garlic in a 7-inch pie pan. Using your hands, break up the sausage into small pieces and spread it evenly throughout the pie pan. Season with the salt and pepper. 2. Slide the wire rack into shelf position 4/5. Place the pan on the wire rack. Select the Bake. Set the temperature to 400°F and the time to 5 minutes. Press Start/Pause to begin cooking. 3. While the sausage cooks, place the cream cheese and broth in a food processor or blender and puree until smooth. 4. Remove the pork from the air fryer and use a fork or metal spatula to crumble it more. Pour the cream cheese mixture into the sausage and stir to combine. Set aside. 5. Make the biscuits: Place the egg whites in a medium-sized mixing bowl or the bowl of a stand mixer and whip with a hand mixer or stand mixer until stiff peaks form. 6. In a separate medium-sized bowl, whisk together the almond flour, salt and baking powder, then cut in the butter. When you are done, the mixture should still have chunks of butter. Gently fold the flour mixture into the egg whites with a rubber spatula. 7. Use a large spoon or ice cream scoop to scoop the dough into 4 equal-sized biscuits, making sure the butter is evenly distributed. Place the biscuits on top of the sausage and cook in the air fryer for 5 minutes, then turn the heat down to 325°F and cook for another 17 to 20 minutes, until the biscuits are golden brown. Serve garnished with fresh thyme leaves. 8. Store leftovers in an airtight container in the refrigerator for up to 3 days. Reheat in a preheated 350°F air fryer for 5 minutes, or until warmed through.

Cheese Spinach Omelet

Prep Time: 5 minutes | Cook Time: 12 minutes | Serves: 2

4 large eggs	2 tablespoons salted butter, melted
1½ cups chopped fresh spinach leaves	½ cup shredded mild Cheddar cheese
2 tablespoons peeled and chopped yellow onion	¼ teaspoon salt

1. In an ungreased 6" round nonstick baking dish, whisk eggs. Stir in spinach, onion, butter, Cheddar, and salt. 2. Slide the wire rack into shelf position 4/5. Place the dish on the wire rack. Select the Bake. Set the temperature to 320°F and the time to 12 minutes. Press Start/Pause to begin cooking. Omelet will be done when browned on the top and firm in the middle. 3. Slice in half and serve warm on two medium plates.

Tasty Cheddar Soufflés

Prep Time: 15 minutes | Cook Time: 12 minutes | Serves: 4

3 large eggs, whites and yolks separated	½ cup shredded sharp Cheddar cheese
¼ teaspoon cream of tartar	3 ounces cream cheese, softened

1. In a large bowl, beat egg whites together with cream of tartar until soft peaks form, about 2 minutes. 2. In a separate medium bowl, beat egg yolks, Cheddar, and cream cheese together until frothy, about 1 minute. Add egg yolk mixture to whites, gently folding until combined. 3. Pour mixture evenly into four 4" ramekins greased with cooking spray. Slide the wire rack into shelf position 4/5. Place the ramekins on the wire rack. Select the Bake. Set the temperature to 350°F and the time to 12 minutes. Press Start/Pause to begin cooking. 4. Eggs will be browned on the top and firm in the center when done. Serve warm.

Super-Easy Bacon Strips

Prep Time: 5 minutes | Cook Time: 12 minutes | Serves: 4

8 slices sugar-free bacon

1. Place the bacon on the Baking Pan and slide the Baking Pan into shelf position 4/5. 2. Select the Bacon setting. Set the cooking temperature to 400°F/204°C and the cooking time to 12 minutes. 3. After 6 minutes, flip bacon and continue cooking time. Serve warm.

Cheese Bacon Quiche

Prep Time: 5 minutes | Cook Time: 12 minutes | Serves: 2

3 large eggs
2 tablespoons heavy whipping cream
¼ teaspoon salt

4 slices cooked sugar-free bacon, crumbled
½ cup shredded mild Cheddar cheese

1. In a large bowl, whisk eggs, cream, and salt together until combined. Mix in bacon and Cheddar. 2. Pour mixture evenly into two ungreased 4" ramekins. Slide the wire rack into shelf position 4/5. Place the ramekins on the wire rack. Select the Bake. Set the temperature to 320°F and the time to 12 minutes. Press Start/Pause to begin cooking. 3. Quiche will be fluffy and set in the middle when done. 4. Let quiche cool in ramekins 5 minutes. Serve warm.

Breakfast Turkey Burgers with Avocado

Prep Time: 5 minutes | Cook Time: 15 minutes | Serves: 4

1-pound ground turkey breakfast sausage
½ teaspoon salt
¼ teaspoon ground black pepper

¼ cup seeded and chopped green bell pepper
2 tablespoons mayonnaise
1 medium avocado, peeled, pitted, and sliced

1. In a large bowl, mix sausage with salt, black pepper, bell pepper, and mayonnaise. Form meat into four patties. 2. Place patties into ungreased Crisper Tray. Slide the Crisper Tray into shelf position 4/5. Select the Air Fry setting. Set the cooking temperature to 370°F and the cooking time to 15 minutes. Press Start/Pause to begin cooking, turning patties halfway through cooking. 3. Burgers will be done when dark brown and they have an internal temperature of at least 165°F. 4. Serve burgers topped with avocado slices on four medium plates.

Simple Mini Bagels

Prep Time: 5 minutes | Cook Time: 10 minutes | Serves: 6

2 cups blanched finely ground almond flour
2 cups shredded mozzarella cheese
3 tablespoons salted butter, divided

1½ teaspoons baking powder
1 teaspoon apple cider vinegar
2 large eggs, divided

1. In a large microwave-safe bowl, combine flour, mozzarella, and 1 tablespoon butter. Microwave on high 90 seconds, then form into a soft ball of dough. 2. Add baking powder, vinegar, and 1 egg to dough, stirring until fully combined. 3. Once dough is cool enough to work with your hands, about 2 minutes, divide evenly into six balls. Poke a hole in each ball of dough with your finger and gently stretch each ball out to be 2" in diameter. 4. In a small microwave-safe bowl, melt remaining butter in microwave on high 30 seconds, then let cool 1 minute. Whisk with remaining egg, then brush mixture over each bagel. 5. Line the Crisper Tray with parchment paper and place bagels onto ungreased parchment, working in batches if needed. 6. Slide the Crisper Tray into shelf position 4/5. Select the Air Fry setting. Set the cooking temperature to 350°F and the cooking time to 10 minutes. Press Start/Pause to begin cooking. Flip them halfway through the cooking time. 7. Allow bagels to set and cool completely, about 15 minutes, before serving. Store leftovers in a sealed bag in the refrigerator up to 4 days.

Breakfast Cheese Meatballs

Prep Time: 10 minutes | Cook Time: 15 minutes | Serves: 3

1-pound ground pork breakfast sausage	½ cup shredded sharp Cheddar cheese
½ teaspoon salt	1-ounce cream cheese, softened
¼ teaspoon ground black pepper	1 large egg, whisked

1. Combine all ingredients in a large bowl. Form mixture into eighteen 1" meatballs. 2. Place meatballs into ungreased Crisper Tray. Slide the Crisper Tray into shelf position 4/5. Select the Air Fry setting. Set the cooking temperature to 400°F and the cooking time to 15 minutes. Press Start/Pause to begin cooking. Shake the tray three times during cooking. 3. Meatballs will be browned on the outside and have an internal temperature of at least 145°F when completely cooked. Serve warm.

Quick Bacon–Wrapped Hot Dog

Prep Time: 5 minutes | Cook Time: 10 minutes | Serves: 4

4 beef hot dogs	4 slices sugar-free bacon

1. Wrap each hot dog with slice of bacon and secure with toothpick. Place on the Baking Pan and slide the Baking Pan into shelf position 4/5. 2. Select the Bacon setting. Set the cooking temperature to 370°F/187°C and the cooking time to 10 minutes. 3. Flip each hot dog halfway through the cooking time. When fully cooked, bacon will be crispy. Serve warm.

Sausage Egg Cups

Prep Time: 10 minutes | Cook Time: 15 minutes | Serves: 6

12 ounces ground pork breakfast sausage	¼ teaspoon ground black pepper
6 large eggs	½ teaspoon crushed red pepper flakes
½ teaspoon salt	

1. Place sausage in six 4" ramekins (about 2 ounces per ramekin) greased with cooking oil. Press sausage down to cover bottom and about ½" up the sides of ramekins. Crack an egg into each ramekin and sprinkle evenly with black pepper, salt, and red pepper flakes. 2. Slide the wire rack into shelf position 4/5. Place the ramekins on the wire rack. Select the Bake. Set the temperature to 350°F and the time to 15 minutes. Press Start/Pause to begin cooking. 3. Egg cups will be done when sausage is fully cooked to at least 145°F and the egg is firm. Serve warm.

Delicious Jalapeño and Bacon Breakfast Pizza

Prep Time: 5 minutes | Cook Time: 10 minutes | Serves: 2

1 cup shredded mozzarella cheese	¼ cup chopped pickled jalapeños
1-ounce cream cheese, broken into small pieces	1 large egg, whisked
4 slices cooked sugar-free bacon, chopped	¼ teaspoon salt

1. Place mozzarella in a single layer on the bottom of an ungreased 6" round nonstick baking dish. Scatter cream cheese pieces, bacon, and jalapeños over mozzarella, then pour egg evenly around baking dish. Sprinkle with salt. 2. Slide the wire rack into shelf position 4/5. Place the baking dish on the wire rack. Select the Bake. Set the temperature to 330°F and the time to 10 minutes. Press Start/Pause to begin cooking. When cheese is brown and egg is set, pizza will be done. 3. Let cool on a large plate 5 minutes before serving.

Savory Pizza Eggs

Prep Time: 5 minutes | Cook Time: 10 minutes | Serves: 2

1 cup shredded mozzarella cheese
7 slices pepperoni, chopped
1 large egg, whisked
¼ teaspoon dried oregano

¼ teaspoon dried parsley
¼ teaspoon garlic powder
¼ teaspoon salt

1. Place mozzarella in a single layer on the bottom of an ungreased 6" round nonstick baking dish. Scatter pepperoni over cheese, then pour egg evenly around baking dish. 2. Sprinkle with remaining ingredients. Slide the wire rack into shelf position 4/5. Place the baking dish on the wire rack. Select the Bake. Set the temperature to 330°F and the time to 10 minutes. Press Start/Pause to begin cooking. When cheese is brown and egg is set, dish will be done. 3. Let cool in dish 5 minutes before serving.

Cheese Jalapeño Egg Cups

Prep Time: 10 minutes | Cook Time: 14 minutes | Serves: 4

4 large eggs
½ teaspoon salt
¼ teaspoon ground black pepper
¼ cup chopped pickled jalapeños

2 ounces cream cheese, softened
¼ teaspoon garlic powder
½ cup shredded sharp Cheddar cheese

1. In a medium bowl, beat eggs together with salt and pepper, then pour evenly into four 4" ramekins greased with cooking spray. 2. In a separate large bowl, mix jalapeños, cream cheese, garlic powder, and Cheddar. Spoon ¼ of the mixture into the center of one ramekin. Repeat with remaining mixture and ramekins. 3. Slide the wire rack into shelf position 4/5. Place the ramekins on the wire rack. Select the Bake. Set the temperature to 320°F and the time to 14 minutes. Press Start/Pause to begin cooking. Eggs will be set when done. Serve warm.

Crunchy Chocolate and Nuts Granola

Prep Time: 10 minutes | Cook Time: 5 minutes | Serves: 6

2 cups pecans, chopped
1 cup unsweetened coconut flakes
1 cup almond slivers
⅓ cup sunflower seeds
¼ cup golden flaxseed

¼ cup low-carb, sugar-free chocolate chips
¼ cup granular erythritol
2 tablespoons unsalted butter
1 teaspoon ground cinnamon

1. In a large bowl, mix all ingredients. 2. Place the mixture into a 4-cup round baking dish. Slide the wire rack into shelf position 4/5. Place the baking dish on the wire rack. Select the Bake. Set the temperature to 320°F and the time to 5 minutes. Press Start/Pause to begin cooking. 3. Allow to cool completely before serving.

Bell Pepper and Ham Egg Cups

Prep Time: 5 minutes | Cook Time: 12 minutes | Serves: 2

4 (1-ounce) slices deli ham
4 large eggs
2 tablespoons full-fat sour cream
¼ cup diced green bell pepper

2 tablespoons diced red bell pepper
2 tablespoons diced white onion
½ cup shredded medium Cheddar cheese

1. Place one slice of ham on the bottom of four baking cups. 2. In a large bowl, whisk the eggs with sour cream. Stir in green pepper, red pepper, and onion. 3. Pour the egg mixture into ham-lined baking cups. Top with Cheddar. 4. Slide the wire rack into shelf position 4/5. Place the cups on the wire rack. Select the Bake. Set the temperature to 320°F and the time to 12 minutes. Press Start/Pause to begin cooking. Cook until the tops are browned. 5. Serve warm.

Bacon–Wrapped Egg Avocado

Prep Time: 5 minutes | Cook Time: 17 minutes | Serves: 1

1 large egg	Fresh parsley, for serving (optional)
1 avocado, halved, peeled, and pitted	Sea salt flakes, for garnish (optional)
2 slices bacon	

1. Spray the Crisper Tray with avocado oil and fill a small bowl with cool water. 2. Place the egg in the Crisper Tray. Slide the Crisper Tray into shelf position 4/5. Place the eggs on the Crisper Tray. 3. Select the Egg setting. Set the cooking temperature to 320°F/160°C and the cooking time to 6 minutes. 4. Cook for 6 minutes for a soft yolk or 7 minutes for a cooked yolk. 5. Transfer the egg to the bowl of cool water and let sit for 2 minutes. Peel and set aside. 6. Use a spoon to carve out extra space in the center of the avocado halves until the cavities are big enough to fit the soft-boiled egg. Place the soft-boiled egg in the center of one half of the avocado and replace the other half of the avocado on top, so the avocado appears whole on the outside. 7. Starting at one end of the avocado, wrap the bacon around the avocado to completely cover it. Use toothpicks to hold the bacon in place. 8. Place the bacon-wrapped avocado on the Baking Pan. Slide the Baking Pan into shelf position 4/5. 9. Select the Bacon setting. Set the cooking temperature to 320°F/160°C and the cooking time to 5 minutes. 10. Flip the avocado over and cook for another 5 minutes, or until the bacon is cooked to your liking. Serve on a bed of fresh parsley, if desired, and sprinkle with salt flakes, if desired. 11. Best served fresh. Store extras in an airtight container in the fridge for up to 4 days. Reheat in the Air Fryer at 320°F/160°C for 4 minutes, or until heated through.

Pepperoni Breakfast Pizza

Prep Time: 5 minutes | Cook Time: 8 minutes | Serves: 1

2 large eggs	¼ cup diced onions
¼ cup unsweetened, unflavored almond milk (or unflavored hemp milk for nut-free)	¼ cup shredded Parmesan cheese (omit for dairy-free)
	6 pepperoni slices (omit for vegetarian)
¼ teaspoon fine sea salt	¼ teaspoon dried oregano leaves
⅛ teaspoon ground black pepper	¼ cup pizza sauce, warmed, for serving

1. Grease a 6 by 3-inch cake pan that fits in the appliance. 2. In a small bowl, whisk together the almond milk, salt, eggs, and pepper with a fork. Add the onions and stir to mix. Pour the mixture into the greased pan. Top with the cheese (if using), pepperoni slices (if using), and oregano. 3. Slide the Crisper Tray with the pan on top into shelf position 6. Select the Pizza setting. Set the cooking temperature to 350°F/176°C and the cooking time to 8 minutes. Cook until the eggs are cooked to your liking. 4. Loosen the eggs from the sides of the pan with a spatula and place them on a serving plate. Drizzle the pizza sauce on top. Best served fresh.

Classic Denver Omelet

Prep Time: 5 minutes | Cook Time: 8 minutes | Serves: 1

2 large eggs	¼ cup diced green and red bell peppers
¼ cup unsweetened, unflavored almond milk	2 tablespoons diced green onions, plus more for garnish
¼ teaspoon fine sea salt	¼ cup shredded cheddar cheese (about 1 ounce) (omit for dairy-free)
⅛ teaspoon ground black pepper	Quartered cherry tomatoes, for serving (optional)
¼ cup diced ham (omit for vegetarian)	

1. Grease a 6 by 3-inch cake pan that fits in the appliance and set aside. 2. In a small bowl, use a fork to whisk together the eggs, salt, almond milk, and pepper. Add the bell peppers, ham, and green onions. Pour the mixture into the greased pan. Add the cheese on top (if using). 3. Slide the Crisper Tray with the pan on top into shelf position 4/5. Select the Air Fry setting. Set the cooking temperature to 350°F/176°C and the cooking time to 8 minutes. Cook until the eggs are cooked to your liking. 4. Loosen the omelet from the sides of the pan with a spatula and place it on a serving plate. Garnish with green onions and serve with cherry tomatoes, if desired. Best served fresh.

Crispy Double-Dipped Mini Cinnamon Biscuits

Prep Time: 15 minutes | Cook Time: 13 minutes | Serves: 4

2 cups blanched almond flour	¼ cup plus 2 tablespoons (¾ stick) very cold unsalted butter
½ cup Swerve confectioners'-style sweetener or equivalent amount of liquid or powdered sweetener	¼ cup unsweetened, unflavored almond milk
1 teaspoon baking powder	1 large egg
½ teaspoon fine sea salt	1 teaspoon vanilla extract
Glaze:	3 teaspoons ground cinnamon
½ cup Swerve confectioners'-style sweetener or equivalent amount of powdered sweetener	¼ cup heavy cream or unsweetened, unflavored almond milk

1. Line Baking Pan with parchment paper. 2. In a medium-sized bowl, combine together the baking powder, almond flour, sweetener, and salt. Cut the butter into ½-inch squares and add the butter into the dry ingredients with a hand mixer. When you are done, the mixture should still have chunks of butter. 3. In a small bowl, whisk together the egg, almond milk, and vanilla extract until blended. Mix the wet ingredients into the dry ingredients with a fork until large clumps form. Add the cinnamon and swirl it into the dough with your hands. 4. Form the dough into sixteen 1-inch balls and, work in batches if necessary, place them on the prepared Baking Pan, spacing them about ½ inch apart. 5. Slide the Baking Pan into shelf position 4/5. Select the Bake setting. Set the cooking temperature to 350°F/176°C and the cooking time to 10 minutes. Bake until golden, 10 to 13 minutes. Remove and allow to cool on the Baking Pan for at least 5 minutes. 5. While the biscuits are baking, make the glaze: Place the powdered sweetener in a small bowl and slowly stir in the heavy cream with a fork. 6. When the biscuits have cooled somewhat, dip the tops into the glaze, allow it to dry a bit, and then dip again for a thick glaze. 7. Serve warm or at room temperature. Store unglazed biscuits in an airtight container in the refrigerator for up to 3 days or in the freezer for up to a month. Reheat in the Air Fryer at 350°F/176°C for 5 minutes until warmed through, and dip in the glaze as instructed above.

Simple Meritage Eggs

Prep Time: 5 minutes | Cook Time: 8 minutes | Serves: 2

2 teaspoons unsalted butter (or coconut oil for dairy-free), for greasing the ramekins	2 tablespoons heavy cream (or unsweetened, unflavored almond milk for dairy-free)
4 large eggs	3 tablespoons finely grated Parmesan cheese (or Kite Hill brand chive cream cheese style spread, softened, for dairy-free)
2 teaspoons chopped fresh thyme	
½ teaspoon fine sea salt	Fresh thyme leaves, for garnish (optional)
¼ teaspoon ground black pepper	

1. Grease two 4-ounce ramekins with the butter. 2. Crack 2 eggs into each ramekin and divide the salt, thyme, and pepper between the ramekins. Pour 1 tablespoon of the heavy cream into each ramekin. Sprinkle each ramekin with 1½ tablespoons of the Parmesan cheese. 3. Arrange the ramekins on the Crisper Tray and slide the Tray into shelf position 4/5. Select the Air Fry setting. Set the cooking temperature to 400°F/204°C and the cooking time to 8 minutes. Cook for 8 minutes for soft-cooked yolks or longer if you desire a harder yolk. 4. Garnish with a sprinkle of ground black pepper and thyme leaves, if desired. Best served fresh.

Chapter 2 Vegetables and Sides

Crispy Cheese Eggplant Rounds

Prep Time: 40 minutes | Cook Time: 10 minutes | Serves: 4

1 large eggplant, ends trimmed, cut into ½" slices	½ teaspoon paprika
½ teaspoon salt	¼ teaspoon garlic powder
2 ounces Parmesan 100% cheese crisps, finely ground	1 large egg

1. Sprinkle eggplant rounds with salt. Place rounds on a kitchen towel for 30 minutes to draw out excess water. Pat rounds dry. 2. In a medium bowl, mix paprika, cheese crisps, and garlic powder. In a separate medium bowl, whisk egg. Dip each eggplant round in egg, then gently press into cheese crisps to coat both sides. 3. Place eggplant rounds on the Crisper Tray and slide the Tray into shelf position 4/5. Select the Vegetables setting. Set the cooking temperature to 400°F/204°C and the cooking time to 10 minutes. 4. Turn rounds halfway through cooking. Eggplant will be golden and crispy when done. Serve warm.

Roasted Cabbage Steaks

Prep Time: 5 minutes | Cook Time: 10 minutes | Serves: 4

1 small head green cabbage, cored and cut into ½"-thick slices	1 clove garlic, peeled and finely minced
¼ teaspoon salt	½ teaspoon dried thyme
¼ teaspoon ground black pepper	½ teaspoon dried parsley
2 tablespoons olive oil	

1. Sprinkle each side of cabbage with salt and pepper. Place the cabbage on the Crisper Tray and slide the Tray into shelf position 4/5, working in batches if needed. 2. Drizzle each side of cabbage with olive oil and sprinkle with remaining ingredients on both sides. Select the Vegetables setting. Set the cooking temperature to 350°F/176°C and the cooking time to 10 minutes. 3. Turn "steaks" halfway through cooking. Cabbage will be browned at the edges and tender when done. Serve warm.

Cauliflower–Pumpkin Casserole with Pecan Topping

Prep Time: 15 minutes | Cook Time: 55 minutes | Serves: 6

2 cups cauliflower florets	of liquid or powdered sweetener
1 cup chicken broth or water	¼ cup unsweetened, unflavored almond milk or heavy cream
1 cup canned pumpkin puree	2 large eggs, beaten
⅓ cup unsalted butter, melted (or coconut oil for dairy-free), plus more for the pan	1 teaspoon fine sea salt
	1 teaspoon vanilla extract
¼ cup Swerve confectioners'-style sweetener or equivalent amount	
Topping:	
1 cup chopped pecans	of powdered sweetener
½ cup blanched almond flour or pecan meal	⅓ cup unsalted butter, melted (or coconut oil for dairy-free)
½ cup Swerve confectioners'-style sweetener or equivalent amount	Chopped fresh parsley leaves, for garnish (optional)

1. Place the cauliflower florets in a casserole dish that will fit in your air fryer. Add the broth to the casserole. 2. Slide the Wire Rack into shelf position 6. Place the casserole dish on the Wire Rack. Select the Bake setting. Set the cooking temperature to 350°F and the cooking time to 20 minutes. Press Start/Pause to begin cooking. Cook until the cauliflower is very tender. 3. Drain the cauliflower and transfer it to a food processor. Set the casserole dish aside; you'll use it in the next step. Blend the cauliflower until very smooth. Add the pumpkin, butter, sweetener, almond milk, eggs, salt, and vanilla and puree until smooth. 4. Grease the casserole that you cooked the cauliflower in with butter. Pour the cauliflower-pumpkin mixture into the casserole. Set aside. 5. Make the topping: In a large bowl, mix together all the ingredients for the topping until well combined. Crumble the topping over the cauliflower-pumpkin mixture. 6. Cook in the air fryer for about 30 to 35 minutes, until cooked through and golden brown on top. Garnish with fresh parsley before serving, if desired. 7. Store leftovers in an airtight container in the fridge for up to 4 days or in the freezer for up to a month. Reheat in a preheated 350°F air fryer for 6 minutes, or until heated through.

Roasted Cauliflower

Prep Time: 5 minutes | Cook Time: 12 minutes | Serves: 4

4 cups cauliflower florets
2 tablespoons dried parsley
1 tablespoon plus 1 teaspoon onion powder
2 teaspoons garlic powder
1½ teaspoons dried dill weed

1 teaspoon dried chives
1 teaspoon fine sea salt or smoked salt
1 teaspoon ground black pepper
Ranch Dressing, for serving (optional)

1. Place the cauliflower in a large bowl and spray it with avocado oil. 2. Place the parsley, onion powder, garlic powder, dill weed, chives, salt, and pepper in a small bowl and stir to combine well. Sprinkle the ranch seasoning over the cauliflower. 3. Place the cauliflower in the Crisper Tray. Slide the Crisper Tray into shelf position 4/5. Select the Vegetables setting. Set the cooking temperature to 400°F and the cooking time to 12 minutes. Press Start/Pause to begin cooking. Cook until tender and crisp on the edges. Serve with the ranch dressing for dipping, if desired. 4. Store leftovers in an airtight container in the fridge for up to 4 days or in the freezer for up to a month. Reheat in a preheated 400°F air fryer for 5 minutes, or until crisp.

White Cheddar Mushroom Soufflés

Prep Time: 15 minutes | Cook Time: 12 minutes | Serves: 4

3 large eggs, whites and yolks separated
½ cup sharp white Cheddar cheese
3 ounces cream cheese, softened
¼ teaspoon cream of tartar

¼ teaspoon salt
¼ teaspoon ground black pepper
½ cup cremini mushrooms, sliced

1. In a large bowl, beat egg whites until stiff peaks form, about 2 minutes. In a separate large bowl, beat Cheddar, cream cheese, cream of tartar, salt, egg yolks, and pepper together until combined. 2. Fold egg whites into cheese mixture, being careful not to stir. Fold in mushrooms and pour mixture evenly into four ungreased 4" ramekins. 3. Place ramekins on the Crisper Tray and slide the Tray into shelf position 4/5. 4. Select the Vegetables setting. Set the cooking temperature to 350°F/176°C and the cooking time to 12 minutes. 5. Eggs will be browned on the top and firm in the center when done. Serve warm.

Spinach Artichoke Cheese Tart

Prep Time: 10 minutes | Cook Time: 40 minutes | Serves: 6

Crust:
1 cup blanched almond flour
1 cup grated Parmesan cheese (about 3 ounces)
Filling:
4 ounces cream cheese (½ cup), softened
1 (8-ounce) package frozen chopped spinach, thawed and drained
½ cup artichoke hearts, drained and chopped
⅓ cup shredded Parmesan cheese, plus more for topping

1 large egg

1 large egg
1 clove garlic, minced
¼ teaspoon fine sea salt

1. Make the crust: Place the almond flour and cheese in a large bowl and mix until well combined. Add the egg and mix until the dough is well combined and stiff. 2. Press the dough into a 6-inch pie pan. Slide the wire rack into shelf position 4/5. Place the pie pan on the wire rack. Select the Bake. Set the temperature to 350°F and the time to 10 minutes. Press Start/Pause to begin cooking. Bake until it starts to brown lightly. 3. Meanwhile, make the filling: Place the cream cheese in a large bowl and stir to break it up. Add the spinach, artichoke hearts, cheese, egg, garlic, and salt. Stir well to combine. 4. Pour the spinach mixture into the prebaked crust and sprinkle with additional Parmesan. Place in the air fryer and cook for 25 to 30 minutes, until cooked through. 5. Store leftovers in an airtight container in the fridge for up to 4 days or in the freezer for up to a month. Reheat in a preheated 350°F air fryer for 5 minutes, or until heated through.

Delicious Eggplant Parmesan

Prep Time: 40 minutes | Cook Time: 17 minutes | Serves: 4

1 medium eggplant, ends trimmed, sliced into ½" rounds	1 ounce 100% cheese crisps, finely crushed
¼ teaspoon salt	½ cup low-carb marinara sauce
2 tablespoons coconut oil	½ cup shredded mozzarella cheese
½ cup grated Parmesan cheese	

1. Sprinkle eggplant rounds with salt on both sides and wrap in a kitchen towel for 30 minutes. Press to remove excess water and drizzle rounds with coconut oil on both sides. 2. In a medium bowl, mix Parmesan and cheese crisps. Press each eggplant slice into mixture to coat both sides. 3. Place rounds on the Crisper Tray and slide the Tray into shelf position 4/5. Select the Vegetables setting. Set the cooking temperature to 350°F/176°C and the cooking time to 15 minutes. 4. Turn rounds halfway through cooking. They will be crispy around the edges when done. 5. When the cooking is complete, spoon marinara over rounds and sprinkle with mozzarella. Continue cooking for another 2 minutes at 350°F/176°C until cheese is melted. Serve warm.

Cheesy Zucchini Fritters

Prep Time: 45 minutes | Cook Time: 12 minutes | Serves: 4

1½ medium zucchini, trimmed and grated	¼ teaspoon garlic powder
½ teaspoon salt, divided	¼ cup grated Parmesan cheese
1 large egg, whisked	

1. Place grated zucchini on a kitchen towel and sprinkle with ¼ teaspoon salt. Wrap in towel and let sit 30 minutes and wring out as much excess moisture as possible. 2. Place zucchini into a large bowl and mix with egg, garlic powder, remaining salt, and Parmesan. Cut a piece of parchment to fit Crisper Tray. Divide mixture into four mounds, about ⅓ cup each, and press out into 4" rounds on ungreased parchment. 3. Place parchment with rounds on the Crisper Tray and slide the Tray into shelf position 4/5. Select the Vegetables setting. Set the cooking temperature to 400°F/204°C and the cooking time to 12 minutes. 4. Turn fritters halfway through cooking. Fritters will be crispy on the edges and tender but firm in the center when done. Serve warm.

Crunchy–Top Cheese Cauliflower

Prep Time: 10 minutes | Cook Time: 15 minutes | Serves: 4

2 cups frozen chopped cauliflower, thawed	2 tablespoons finely diced onions
2 ounces cream cheese (¼ cup), softened	3 tablespoons beef broth
¼ cup shredded Gruyère or Swiss cheese	¼ teaspoon fine sea salt
¼ cup shredded sharp cheddar cheese	
Topping:	
¼ cup pork dust	4 slices bacon, finely diced
¼ cup unsalted butter, melted, plus more for greasing ramekins	
For Garnish (optional):	
Chopped fresh thyme or chives	

1. Place the cauliflower on a paper towel and pat dry. Cut any large pieces of cauliflower into ½-inch pieces. 2. In a medium bowl, stir together the cream cheese, Gruyère, cheddar, and onions. Slowly stir in the broth and combine well. Add the salt and stir to combine. Add the cauliflower and stir gently to mix the cauliflower into the cheese sauce. 3. Grease four 4-ounce ramekins with butter. Divide the cauliflower mixture among the ramekins, filling each three-quarters full. 4. Make the topping: In a small bowl, stir together the pork dust, butter, and bacon until well combined. Divide the topping among the ramekins. 5. Slide the wire rack into shelf position 4/5. Place the ramekins on the wire rack. Select the Bake. Set the temperature to 375°F and the time to 15 minutes. Press Start/Pause to begin cooking. Cook until the topping is browned and the bacon is crispy. 6. Garnish with fresh thyme or chives, if desired. 7. Store leftovers in the ramekins covered with foil. Reheat in a preheated 375°F air fryer for 6 minutes, or until the cauliflower is heated through and the top is crispy.

Butter Roasted Spaghetti Squash

Prep Time: 10 minutes | Cook Time: 45 minutes | Serves: 6

1 (4-pound) spaghetti squash, halved and seeded
2 tablespoons coconut oil
4 tablespoons salted butter, melted

1 teaspoon garlic powder
2 teaspoons dried parsley

1. Brush shell of spaghetti squash with coconut oil. Brush inside with butter. Sprinkle inside with garlic powder and parsley. 2. Place squash skin side down on the Crisper Tray and slide the Tray into shelf position 4/5, working in batches if needed. 3. Select the Vegetables setting. Set the cooking temperature to 350°F/176°C and the cooking time to 30 minutes. 4. When the cooking is complete, flip squash and cook for an additional 15 minutes until fork-tender. 5. Use a fork to remove spaghetti strands from shell and serve warm.

Homemade Alfredo Eggplant Stacks

Prep Time: 5 minutes | Cook Time: 12 minutes | Serves: 6

1 large eggplant, ends trimmed, cut into ¼" slices
1 medium beefsteak tomato, cored and cut into ¼" slices
1 cup Alfredo sauce

8 ounces fresh mozzarella cheese, cut into 18 slices
2 tablespoons fresh parsley leaves

1. Place 6 slices eggplant in bottom of an ungreased 6" round nonstick baking dish that fits in the appliance. Place 1 slice tomato on top of each eggplant round, followed by 1 tablespoon Alfredo and 1 slice mozzarella. Repeat with remaining ingredients, about three repetitions. 2. Cover dish with aluminum foil. Slide the Crisper Tray with the dish on top into shelf position 4/5. 3. Select the Vegetables setting. Set the cooking temperature to 350°F/176°C and the cooking time to 12 minutes. 4. Eggplant will be tender when done. Sprinkle parsley evenly over each stack. Serve warm.

Herb–Roasted Radishes with Parmesan cheese

Prep Time: 10 minutes | Cook Time: 10 minutes | Serves: 6

1 pound radishes, ends removed, quartered
2 tablespoons salted butter, melted
½ teaspoon garlic powder
½ teaspoon dried parsley

¼ teaspoon dried oregano
¼ teaspoon ground black pepper
¼ cup grated Parmesan cheese

1. Place radishes into a medium bowl and drizzle with butter. Sprinkle with garlic powder, parsley, oregano, and pepper, then place into ungreased Crisper Tray. 2. Slide the Crisper Tray into shelf position 4/5. Select the Vegetables setting. Set the cooking temperature to 350°F and the cooking time to 10 minutes. Press Start/Pause to begin cooking. Shake the tray three times during cooking. Radishes will be done when tender and golden. 3. Place radishes into a large serving dish and sprinkle with Parmesan. Serve warm.

Air Fryer Garlic Thyme Mushrooms

Prep Time: 5 minutes | Cook Time: 10 minutes | Serves: 4

3 tablespoons unsalted butter (or coconut oil for dairy-free), melted
1 (8-ounce) package button mushrooms, sliced
2 cloves garlic, minced

3 sprigs fresh thyme leaves, plus more for garnish
½ teaspoon fine sea salt

1. Spray the Crisper Tray with avocado oil. 2. Place all the ingredients in a medium-sized bowl. Use a spoon or your hands to coat the mushroom slices. 3. Place the mushrooms in the Crisper Tray in one layer; work in batches if necessary. 4. Slide the Crisper Tray into shelf position 4/5. Select the Air Fry setting. Set the cooking temperature to 400°F and the cooking time to 10 minutes. Press Start/Pause to begin cooking. Cook until slightly crispy and brown. Garnish with thyme sprigs before serving. 5. Store leftovers in an airtight container in the fridge for up to 5 days or in the freezer for up to a month. 6. Reheat in a preheated 350°F air fryer for 5 minutes, or until heated through.

Parmesan Flan with Cherry Tomatoes

Prep Time: 10 minutes | Cook Time: 25 minutes | Serves: 4

½ cup grated Parmesan cheese (about 1½ ounces)	⅛ teaspoon ground white pepper
1 cup heavy cream, very warm	1 large egg
⅛ teaspoon fine sea salt	1 large egg yolk
For Serving/Garnish (optional):	
2 cups arugula	4 slices Italian cured beef (omit for vegetarian)
1 cup heirloom cherry tomatoes, halved	Ground black pepper

1. Grease four 4-ounce ramekins well. 2. Place the Parmesan in a medium-sized bowl and pour in the warm cream. Stir well to combine and add the salt and pepper. 3. In a separate medium-sized bowl, beat the egg and yolk until well combined. Gradually stir in the warm Parmesan mixture. 4. Pour the egg-and-cheese mixture into the prepared ramekins, cover the ramekins with foil, and place them in a casserole dish that will fit in your air fryer. 5. Pour boiling water into the casserole dish until the water reaches halfway up the sides of the ramekins. 6. Slide the Wire Rack into shelf position 6. Place the casserole dish on the Wire Rack. Select the Bake setting. Set the cooking temperature to 350°F and the cooking time to 25 minutes. Press Start/Pause to begin cooking. Bake until the flan is just set. Check after 20 minutes. 7. Let the flan rest for 15 minutes. Serve with arugula, halved cherry tomatoes, and slices of Italian cured beef, if desired. Garnish with ground black pepper, if desired. 8. Store leftovers in an airtight container in the fridge for up to 5 days. Reheat the flan in a ramekin in a preheated 350°F air fryer for 5 minutes, or until heated through.

Tomato–Stuffed Zucchini Boats

Prep Time: 5 minutes | Cook Time: 10 minutes | Serves: 4

1 large zucchini, ends removed, halved lengthwise	¼ cup feta cheese
6 grape tomatoes, quartered	1 tablespoon balsamic vinegar
¼ teaspoon salt	1 tablespoon olive oil

1. Use a spoon to scoop out 2 tablespoons from center of each zucchini half, making just enough space to fill with tomatoes and feta. 2. Place tomatoes evenly in centers of zucchini halves and sprinkle with salt. Place the zucchini halves into the Crisper Tray. Slide the Crisper Tray into shelf position 4/5. Select the Vegetables setting. Set the cooking temperature to 350°F and the cooking time to 10 minutes. Press Start/Pause to begin cooking. When done, zucchini will be tender. 3. Transfer boats to a serving tray and sprinkle with feta, then drizzle with vinegar and olive oil. Serve warm.

Lime Gingered Cauliflower Rice

Prep Time: 5 minutes | Cook Time: 8 minutes | Serves: 4

2 cups cauliflower florets	1 teaspoon grated fresh ginger
⅓ cup sliced green onions, plus more for garnish	1 teaspoon fish sauce or fine sea salt
3 tablespoons wheat-free tamari or coconut aminos	1 teaspoon lime juice
1 garlic clove, smashed to a paste or minced	⅛ teaspoon ground black pepper

1. Place the cauliflower in a food processor and pulse until it resembles grains of rice. 2. Place all the ingredients, including the riced cauliflower, in a large bowl and stir well to combine. 3. Transfer the cauliflower mixture to a 6-inch pie pan that will fit in your air fryer. 4. Slide the wire rack into shelf position 4/5. Place the pie pan on the wire rack. Select the Bake. Set the temperature to 375°F and the time to 8 minutes. Press Start/Pause to begin cooking. Cook until soft, shaking halfway through. Garnish with sliced green onions before serving. 5. Store leftovers in an airtight container in the fridge for up to 4 days. Reheat in a preheated 375°F air fryer for 4 minutes, or until heated through.

Roasted Broccoli & Almonds Salad

Prep Time: 5 minutes | Cook Time: 7 minutes | Serves: 4

2 cups fresh broccoli florets, chopped
1 tablespoon olive oil
¼ teaspoon salt
⅛ teaspoon ground black pepper

¼ cup lemon juice, divided
¼ cup shredded Parmesan cheese
¼ cup sliced roasted almonds

1. In a large bowl, toss broccoli and olive oil together. Sprinkle with salt and black pepper, then drizzle with 2 tablespoons lemon juice. 2. Place broccoli into the Crisper Tray. Slide the Crisper Tray into shelf position 4/5. Select the Vegetables setting. Set the cooking temperature to 350°F and the cooking time to 7 minutes. Press Start/Pause to begin cooking, shaking the tray halfway through cooking. Broccoli will be golden on the edges when done. 3. Place broccoli into a large serving bowl and drizzle with remaining lemon juice. Sprinkle with Parmesan and almonds. Serve warm.

Bacon–Jalapeño Cheese Sticks

Prep Time: 10 minutes | Cook Time: 15 minutes | Serves: 4

2 cups shredded mozzarella cheese
¼ cup grated Parmesan cheese
¼ cup chopped pickled jalapeños

2 large eggs, whisked
4 slices cooked sugar-free bacon, chopped

1. Mix all ingredients together in a large bowl. Cut a piece of parchment paper to fit inside the Crisper Tray. 2. Dampen your hands with a bit of water and press out mixture into a circle to fit on ungreased parchment. You may need to separate into two smaller circles, depending on the size of air fryer. 3. Slide the Crisper Tray into shelf position 4/5. Select the Vegetables setting. Set the cooking temperature to 320°F and the cooking time to 15 minutes. Press Start/Pause to begin cooking. Carefully flip when 5 minutes remain on timer. The top will be golden brown when done. Slice into eight sticks. Serve warm.

Simple Fried Green Beans

Prep Time: 5 minutes | Cook Time: 8 minutes | Serves: 4

2 teaspoons olive oil
½ pound fresh green beans, ends trimmed

¼ teaspoon salt
¼ teaspoon ground black pepper

1. In a large bowl, drizzle olive oil over green beans and sprinkle with salt and pepper. 2. Place green beans into ungreased Crisper Tray. 3. Slide the Crisper Tray into shelf position 4/5. Select the Vegetables setting. Set the cooking temperature to 350°F and the cooking time to 8 minutes. Press Start/Pause to begin cooking. Shake the tray two times during cooking. Green beans will be dark golden and crispy at the edges when done. Serve warm.

Sweet Pepper Poppers

Prep Time: 10 minutes | Cook Time: 8 minutes | Serves: 4

4 ounces cream cheese, softened
1 cup chopped fresh spinach leaves
½ teaspoon garlic powder

8 mini sweet bell peppers, tops removed, seeded, and halved lengthwise

1. In a medium bowl, mix cream cheese, spinach, and garlic powder. Place 1 tablespoon mixture into each sweet pepper half and press down to smooth. 2. Place poppers into ungreased Crisper Tray. 3. Slide the Crisper Tray into shelf position 4/5. Select the Vegetables setting. Set the cooking temperature to 400°F and the cooking time to 8 minutes. Press Start/Pause to begin cooking. 4. Poppers will be done when cheese is browned on top and peppers are tender-crisp. Serve warm.

Roasted Garlicky Brussels Sprouts

Prep Time: 5 minutes | Cook Time: 10 minutes | Serves: 6

1 pound fresh Brussels sprouts, trimmed and halved	¼ teaspoon ground black pepper
2 tablespoons coconut oil	½ teaspoon garlic powder
½ teaspoon salt	1 tablespoon salted butter, melted

1. Place Brussels sprouts into a large bowl. Drizzle with coconut oil and sprinkle with salt, pepper, and garlic powder. 2. Place Brussels sprouts into ungreased Crisper Tray. 3. Slide the Crisper Tray into shelf position 4/5. Select the Vegetables setting. Set the cooking temperature to 350°F and the cooking time to 10 minutes. Press Start/Pause to begin cooking. Shake the tray three times during cooking. Brussels sprouts will be dark golden and tender when done. 4. Place cooked sprouts in a large serving dish and drizzle with butter. Serve warm.

Lemony Cauliflower Steaks

Prep Time: 5 minutes | Cook Time: 15 minutes | Serves: 4

1 small head cauliflower, leaves and core removed, cut into 4 (½"-thick) "steaks"	¼ teaspoon salt
4 tablespoons olive oil, divided	⅛ teaspoon ground black pepper
1 medium lemon, zested and juiced, divided	1 tablespoon salted butter, melted
	1 tablespoon capers, rinsed

1. Brush each cauliflower "steak" with ½ tablespoon olive oil on both sides and sprinkle with lemon zest, salt, and pepper on both sides. 2. Place cauliflower into ungreased Crisper Tray. 3. Slide the Crisper Tray into shelf position 4/5. Select the Vegetables setting. Set the cooking temperature to 400°F and the cooking time to 15 minutes. Press Start/Pause to begin cooking, turning cauliflower halfway through cooking. Steaks will be golden at the edges and browned when done. 4. Transfer steaks to four medium plates. In a small bowl, whisk remaining olive oil, butter, lemon juice, and capers, and pour evenly over steaks. Serve warm.

Cheesy Cauliflower Rice—Stuffed Bell Peppers

Prep Time: 10 minutes | Cook Time: 15 minutes | Serves: 4

2 cups uncooked cauliflower rice	¼ teaspoon salt
¾ cup drained canned petite diced tomatoes	¼ teaspoon ground black pepper
2 tablespoons olive oil	4 medium green bell peppers, tops removed, seeded
1 cup shredded mozzarella cheese	

1. In a large bowl, mix all ingredients except bell peppers. Scoop mixture evenly into peppers. 2. Place peppers into ungreased Crisper Tray. 3. Slide the Crisper Tray into shelf position 4/5. Select the Air Fry setting. Set the cooking temperature to 350°F and the cooking time to 15 minutes. Press Start/Pause to begin cooking. 4. Peppers will be tender and cheese will be melted when done. Serve warm.

Zucchini and Spinach Stuffed Portobellos

Prep Time: 10 minutes | Cook Time: 8 minutes | Serves: 4

3 ounces cream cheese, softened	4 large portobello mushrooms, stems removed
½ medium zucchini, trimmed and chopped	2 tablespoons coconut oil, melted
¼ cup seeded and chopped red bell pepper	½ teaspoon salt
1½ cups chopped fresh spinach leaves	

1. In a medium bowl, mix cream cheese, zucchini, pepper, and spinach. 2. Drizzle mushrooms with coconut oil and sprinkle with salt. Scoop ¼ zucchini mixture into each mushroom. 3. Place mushrooms into the Crisper Tray. Slide the Crisper Tray into shelf position 4/5. Select the Air Fry setting. Set the cooking temperature to 400°F and the cooking time to 8 minutes. Press Start/Pause to begin cooking. 4. Portobellos will be tender and tops will be browned when done. Serve warm.

Zucchini–Mushroom Burgers

Prep Time: 10 minutes | Cook Time: 12 minutes | Serves: 4

8 ounces cremini mushrooms
2 large egg yolks
½ medium zucchini, trimmed and chopped
¼ cup peeled and chopped yellow onion

1 clove garlic, peeled and finely minced
½ teaspoon salt
¼ teaspoon ground black pepper

1. Place all ingredients into a food processor and pulse twenty times until finely chopped and combined. 2. Separate the mixture into four equal sections and press each into a burger shape. Place burgers into ungreased Crisper Tray. 3. Slide the Crisper Tray into shelf position 4/5. Select the Air Fry setting. Set the cooking temperature to 375°F and the cooking time to 12 minutes. Press Start/Pause to begin cooking, turning burgers halfway through cooking. Burgers will be browned and firm when done. 4. Place burgers on a large plate and let cool 5 minutes before serving.

Cheese Broccoli Sticks with Ranch Dressing

Prep Time: 10 minutes | Cook Time: 16 minutes | Serves: 2

1 (10-ounce) steamer bag broccoli florets, cooked according to
package instructions
1 large egg
1-ounce Parmesan 100% cheese crisps, finely ground

½ cup shredded sharp Cheddar cheese
½ teaspoon salt
½ cup ranch dressing

1. Let cooked broccoli cool 5 minutes, then place into a food processor with egg, cheese crisps, Cheddar, and salt. Process on low for 30 seconds until all ingredients are combined and begin to stick together. 2. Cut a sheet of parchment paper to fit the Crisper Tray. Take one scoop of mixture, about 3 tablespoons, and roll into a 4" stick shape, pressing down gently to flatten the top. Place stick on ungreased parchment into the Crisper Tray. Repeat with remaining mixture to form eight sticks. 3. Slide the Crisper Tray into shelf position 4/5. Select the Air Fry setting. Set the cooking temperature to 350°F and the cooking time to 16 minutes. Press Start/Pause to begin cooking. Flip them halfway through the cooking time. Sticks will be golden brown when done. 4. Serve warm with ranch dressing on the side for dipping.

Best Cheesy Baked Asparagus

Prep Time: 10 minutes | Cook Time: 18 minutes | Serves: 4

½ cup heavy whipping cream
½ cup grated Parmesan cheese
2 ounces cream cheese, softened

1 pound asparagus, ends trimmed, chopped into 1" pieces
¼ teaspoon salt
¼ teaspoon ground black pepper

1. In a medium bowl, whisk together Parmesan, heavy cream, and cream cheese until combined. 2. Place asparagus into an ungreased 6" round nonstick baking dish that fits in the appliance. Add cheese mixture over top and sprinkle with pepper and salt. 3. Slide the Crisper Tray with the dish on top into shelf position 4/5. Select the Vegetables setting. Set the cooking temperature to 350°F/176°C and the cooking time to 18 minutes. Asparagus will be tender when done. Serve warm.

Dijon Roasted Cabbage

Prep Time: 10 minutes | Cook Time: 10 minutes | Serves: 4

1 small head cabbage, cored and sliced into 1"-thick slices
2 tablespoons olive oil, divided
½ teaspoon salt

1 tablespoon Dijon mustard
1 teaspoon apple cider vinegar
1 teaspoon granular erythritol

1. Drizzle each cabbage slice with 1 tablespoon olive oil and sprinkle with salt. Place slices on the Crisper Tray and slide the Tray into shelf position 4/5, working in batches if needed. 2. Select the Vegetables setting. Set the cooking temperature to 350°F/176°C and the cooking time to 10 minutes. Cabbage will be tender and edges will begin to brown when done. 3. In a small bowl, whisk remaining olive oil, mustard, vinegar, and erythritol. Drizzle over cabbage in a large serving dish. Serve warm.

Crispy Bacon–Wrapped Asparagus

Prep Time: 5 minutes | Cook Time: 10 minutes | Serves: 4

1-pound asparagus, trimmed (about 24 spears)	½ cup Ranch Dressing, for serving
4 slices bacon or beef bacon	2 tablespoons chopped fresh chives, for garnish

1. Spray the Crisper Tray with avocado oil. 2. Slice the bacon down the middle, making long and thin strips. Wrap 1 slice of bacon around 3 asparagus spears and secure each end with a toothpick. Repeat with the remaining bacon and asparagus. 3. Place the asparagus bundles in the Crisper Tray in a single layer. Slide the Crisper Tray into shelf position 4/5. Select the Air Fry setting. Set the cooking temperature to 400°F and the cooking time to 10 minutes. Press Start/Pause to begin cooking. Cook until the asparagus is slightly charred on the ends and the bacon is crispy. 4. Serve with ranch dressing and garnish with chives. Best served fresh. Store leftovers in an airtight container in the fridge for up to 5 days. Reheat in a preheated 400°F air fryer for 3 minutes, or until heated through.

Perfect Zucchini Noodles

Prep Time: 5 minutes | Cook Time: 8 minutes | Serves: 2

1 (12-inch) zucchini
Special Equipment:
Spiral slicer

1. Spray the Crisper Tray with avocado oil. 2. Cut the ends off the zucchini to create nice even edges. If you desire completely white noodles, peel the zucchini. Using a spiral slicer, cut the zucchini into long, thin noodles. 3. Spread out the zucchini noodles on the Crisper Tray in a single layer and slide the Crisper Tray into shelf position 4/5. Select the Vegetables setting. Set the cooking temperature to 400°F/204°C and the cooking time to 8 minutes. Cook until soft. Remove and serve immediately. 4. Store leftovers in an airtight container for 4 days. Reheat in the Air Fryer at 400°F/204°C for 3 minutes, or until heated through.

Jalapeño and Cheese Cauliflower Mash

Prep Time: 10 minutes | Cook Time: 15 minutes | Serves: 6

1 (12-ounce) steamer bag cauliflower florets, cooked according to package instructions	½ cup shredded sharp Cheddar cheese
2 tablespoons salted butter, softened	¼ cup pickled jalapeños
2 ounces cream cheese, softened	½ teaspoon salt
	¼ teaspoon ground black pepper

1. Place cooked cauliflower into a food processor with remaining ingredients. Pulse twenty times until cauliflower is smooth and all ingredients are combined. 2. Spoon mash into an ungreased 6" round nonstick baking dish that fits in the appliance. Slide the Crisper Tray with the dish on top into shelf position 4/5. Select the Vegetables setting. Set the cooking temperature to 380°F/193°C and the cooking time to 15 minutes. 3. The top will be golden brown when done. Serve warm.

Italian Burrata–Stuffed Tomatoes

Prep Time: 5 minutes | Cook Time: 5 minutes | Serves: 4

4 medium tomatoes	Fresh basil leaves, for garnish
½ teaspoon fine sea salt	Extra-virgin olive oil, for drizzling
4 (2-ounce) Burrata balls	

1. Core the tomatoes and scoop out the seeds and membranes using a melon baller or spoon. Sprinkle the insides of the tomatoes with salt. 2. Stuff each tomato with a ball of Burrata. Place tomato on the Baking Pan and slide the Pan into shelf position 4/5. Select the Vegetables setting. Set the cooking temperature to 300°F/148°C and the cooking time to 5 minutes. Cook until the cheese has softened. 3. Garnish with basil leaves and drizzle with olive oil. Serve warm. 4. Store leftovers in an airtight container in the refrigerator for up to 4 days. Reheat in the Air Fryer at 300°F/148°C for about 3 minutes, until heated through.

Roasted Brussels Sprouts

Prep Time: 5 minutes | Cook Time: 8 minutes | Serves: 4

2 cups Brussels sprouts, trimmed and halved
3 tablespoons ghee or coconut oil, melted
1 teaspoon fine sea salt or smoked salt
Dash of lime or lemon juice

Thinly sliced Parmesan cheese, for serving (optional; omit for dairy-free)
Lemon slices, for serving (optional)

1. In a large bowl, toss together the Brussels sprouts, ghee, and salt. Add the lime or lemon juice. 2. Place the Brussels sprouts on the Crisper Tray and slide the Tray into shelf position 4/5. Select the Vegetables setting. Set the cooking temperature to 400°F/204°C and the cooking time to 8 minutes. Cook until crispy, shaking after 5 minutes. Serve with thinly sliced Parmesan and lemon slices, if desired. 3. Best served fresh. Store leftovers in an airtight container in the fridge for up to 5 days. Reheat in the Air Fryer at 390°F/198°C for 3 minutes, or until heated through.

Creamy Buffalo Chicken Dip

Prep Time: 10 minutes | Cook Time: 12 minutes | Serves: 8

8 ounces cream cheese, softened
2 cups chopped cooked chicken thighs

½ cup buffalo sauce
1 cup shredded mild Cheddar cheese, divided

1. In a large bowl, combine chicken, buffalo sauce, cream cheese, and ½ cup Cheddar. Scoop dip into an ungreased 4-cup nonstick baking dish that fits in the appliance and top with remaining Cheddar. 2. Slide the Crisper Tray with the dish on top into shelf position 4/5. Select the Air Fry setting. Set the cooking temperature to 375°F/190°C and the cooking time to 12 minutes. 3. Dip will be browned on top and bubbling when done. Serve warm.

Cheesy Pepperoni Rolls

Prep Time: 5 minutes | Cook Time: 8 minutes | Serves: 12

2½ cups shredded mozzarella cheese
2 ounces cream cheese, softened
1 cup blanched finely ground almond flour

48 slices pepperoni
2 teaspoons Italian seasoning

1. In a large microwave-safe bowl, combine mozzarella, cream cheese, and flour. Microwave on high 90 seconds until cheese is melted. 2. Using a wooden spoon, mix melted mixture 2 minutes until a dough forms. 3. Once dough is cool enough to work with your hands, about 2 minutes, spread it out into a 12" × 4" rectangle on ungreased parchment paper. Line dough with pepperoni, divided into four even rows. Sprinkle Italian seasoning evenly over pepperoni. 4. Starting at the long end of the dough, roll up until a log is formed. Cut the log into twelve even pieces. 5. Place pizza rolls in an ungreased 6" nonstick baking dish that fits in the appliance. Slide the Crisper Tray with the dish on top into shelf position 4/5. Select the Air Fry setting. Set the cooking temperature to 375°F/190°C and the cooking time to 8 minutes. 6. Rolls will be golden and firm when done. Allow cooked rolls to cool 10 minutes before serving.

Golden Mozzarella Sticks

Prep Time: 15 minutes | Cook Time: 14 minutes | Serves: 12

Dough:
1¾ cups shredded mozzarella cheese (7 ounces)
2 tablespoons unsalted butter
1 large egg, beaten
Spice Mix:
¼ cup grated Parmesan cheese
3 tablespoons garlic powder
For Serving (optional):
½ cup marinara sauce

¾ cup blanched almond flour
⅛ teaspoon fine sea salt
24 pieces of string cheese

1 tablespoon dried oregano leaves
1 tablespoon onion powder

½ cup pesto

1. Make the dough: Place the mozzarella and butter in a large microwave-safe bowl and microwave for 1 to 2 minutes, until the cheese is entirely melted. Stir well. 2. Add the eggs and mix well on low speed with a hand mixer. Add the almond flour and salt and mix well with the mixer. 3. Lay a piece of parchment paper on the countertop and place the dough on it. Knead it for about 3 minutes; the dough should be thick yet pliable. (Note: If the dough is too sticky, chill it in the refrigerator for an hour or overnight.) 4. Scoop up 3 tablespoons of the dough and flatten it into a very thin 3½ by 2-inch rectangle. Place one piece of string cheese in the center and use your hands to press the dough tightly around it. Repeat with the remaining string cheese and dough. 5. In a shallow dish, combine the spice mix ingredients. Place a wrapped piece of string cheese in the dish and roll while pressing down to form a nice crust. Repeat with the remaining pieces of string cheese. Place in the freezer for 2 hours. 6. Ten minutes before air frying, spray the Crisper Tray with avocado oil. 7. Place the frozen mozzarella sticks in the Crisper Tray, leaving space between them. Slide the Crisper Tray into shelf position 4/5. Select the Air Fry setting. Set the cooking temperature to 425°F and the cooking time to 12 minutes. Press Start/Pause to begin cooking. Flip them halfway through the cooking time. Remove from the air fryer and serve with marinara sauce and pesto, if desired. 8. Store leftovers in an airtight container in the refrigerator for up to 3 days or in the freezer for up to a month. Reheat in a preheated 425°F air fryer for 4 minutes, or until warmed through.

Homemade Cauliflower Buns

Prep Time: 15 minutes | Cook Time: 12 minutes | Serves: 8

1 (12-ounce) steamer bag cauliflower, cooked according to package instructions	¼ cup blanched finely ground almond flour
½ cup shredded mozzarella cheese	1 large egg
¼ cup shredded mild Cheddar cheese	½ teaspoon salt

1. Let cooked cauliflower cool about 10 minutes. Use a kitchen towel to wring out excess moisture and then place cauliflower in a food processor. 2. Add mozzarella, flour, egg, Cheddar, and salt to the food processor and pulse twenty times until mixture is combined. It will resemble a soft, wet dough. 3. Divide mixture into eight piles. Wet your hands with water to prevent sticking and press each pile into a flat bun shape, about ½" thick. 4. Cut a sheet of parchment to fit into the Crisper Tray and place the ungreased parchment on the Crisper Tray. Working in batches if needed, place the formed dough on Crisper Tray and slide the Crisper Tray into shelf position 4/5. Select the Air Fry setting. Set the cooking temperature to 350°F/176°C and the cooking time to 12 minutes. Turn the buns halfway through cooking. 5. Let buns cool 10 minutes before serving. Serve warm.

Tasty Mini Greek Meatballs

Prep Time: 10 minutes | Cook Time: 10 minutes | Serves: 6

1 cup fresh spinach leaves	½ teaspoon salt
¼ cup peeled and diced red onion	½ teaspoon ground cumin
½ cup crumbled feta cheese	¼ teaspoon ground black pepper
1 pound 85/15 ground turkey	

1. Place spinach, onion, and feta in a food processor, and pulse ten times until spinach is chopped. Scoop into a large bowl. 2. Add turkey to bowl and sprinkle with salt, cumin, and pepper. Mix until fully combined. Roll mixture into thirty-six meatballs (about 1 tablespoon each). 3. Place meatballs on the Crisper Tray and slide the Tray into shelf position 4/5, working in batches if needed. Select the Air Fry setting. Set the cooking temperature to 350°F/176°C and the cooking time to 10 minutes. Shake twice during cooking. 4. Meatballs will be browned and have an internal temperature of at least 165°F when done. Serve warm.

Corned Beef Prosciutto Rolls

Prep Time: 15 minutes | Cook Time: 10 minutes | Serves: 4

1 (8-ounce) package cream cheese, softened	½ cup shredded Swiss cheese (about 2 ounces)
½ pound cooked corned beef, chopped	20 slices prosciutto
½ cup drained and chopped sauerkraut	
Thousand Island Dipping Sauce:	
¾ cup mayonnaise	⅛ teaspoon fine sea salt
¼ cup chopped dill pickles	Fresh thyme leaves, for garnish
2 tablespoons Swerve confectioners'-style sweetener or equivalent amount of liquid or powdered sweetener	Ground black pepper, for garnish
¼ cup tomato sauce	Sauerkraut, for serving (optional)

1. Spray the Crisper Tray with avocado oil. 2. Make the filling: Place the cream cheese in a medium bowl and stir to break it up. Add the corned beef, sauerkraut, and Swiss cheese and stir well to combine. 3. Assemble the prosciutto rolls: Lay 1 slice of prosciutto on a sushi mat or a sheet of parchment paper with a short end toward you. Lay another slice of prosciutto on top of it at a right angle, forming a cross. Spoon 3 to 4 tablespoons of the filling into the center of the cross. 4. Fold the sides of the top slice up and over the filling to form the ends of the roll. Tightly roll up the long piece of prosciutto, starting at the edge closest to you, into a tight egg roll shape that overlaps by an inch or so. (Note: If the prosciutto rips, it's okay. It will seal when you fry it.) Repeat with the remaining prosciutto and filling. 5. Place the prosciutto rolls in the Crisper Tray seam-side down, leaving space between them. Slide the Crisper Tray into shelf position 4/5. Select the Air Fry setting. Set the cooking temperature to 400°F and the cooking time to 10 minutes. Press Start/Pause to begin cooking. 6. While the prosciutto rolls are cooking, make the dipping sauce: In a small bowl, combine the mayo, pickles, tomato sauce, sweetener, and salt. Stir well and garnish with thyme and ground black pepper. (The dipping sauce can be made up to 3 days ahead.) 7. Serve the prosciutto rolls with the dipping sauce and sauerkraut if desired. Best served fresh. Store leftovers in an airtight container in the refrigerator for up to 5 days or in the freezer for up to a month. Reheat in a preheated 400°F air fryer for 4 minutes, or until heated through and crispy.

Chewy Sweet–Spicy Beef Jerky

Prep Time: 2 hours | Cook Time: 4 hours | Serves: 6

1 pound eye of round beef, fat trimmed, sliced into ¼"-thick strips	½ teaspoon ground black pepper
¼ cup soy sauce	2 tablespoons granular brown erythritol
2 tablespoons sriracha hot chili sauce	

1. Place beef in a large sealable bowl or bag. Pour soy sauce and sriracha into bowl or bag and sprinkle in pepper and erythritol. Shake or stir to combine ingredients and coat steak. Cover and place in refrigerator to marinate at least 2 hours up to overnight. 2. Once marinated, remove strips from marinade and pat dry. Place on the Crisper Tray in a single layer, working in batches if needed, and slide the Tray into shelf position 4/5. Select the Air Fry setting. Set the cooking temperature to 180°F/82°C and cook for 4 hours. 3. Jerky will be chewy and dark brown when done. 4. Store in airtight container in a cool, dry place up to 2 weeks.

Flavorful Ranch Chicken Bites

Prep Time: 10 minutes | Cook Time: 15 minutes | Serves: 6

2 (6-ounce) boneless, skinless chicken breasts, cut into 1" cubes	⅓ cup ranch dressing
1 tablespoon coconut oil	½ cup shredded Colby cheese
½ teaspoon salt	4 slices cooked sugar-free bacon, crumbled
¼ teaspoon ground black pepper	

1. Drizzle chicken with coconut oil. Sprinkle with pepper and salt, and place into an ungreased 6" round nonstick baking dish that fits in the appliance. 2. Slide the Crisper Tray with the dish on top into shelf position 4/5. Select the Air Fry setting. Set the cooking temperature to 370°F/187°C and the cooking time to 10 minutes. Stir chicken halfway through cooking. 3. When the cooking is complete, drizzle ranch dressing over chicken and top with Colby and bacon. 4. Adjust the temperature to 400°F/204°C and cook for 5 minutes. 5. When done, chicken will be browned and have an internal temperature of at least 165°F. Serve warm.

Spicy Blooming Onion

Prep Time: 10 minutes | Cook Time: 35 minutes | Serves: 8

1 extra-large onion (about 3 inches in diameter)	2 teaspoons paprika
2 large eggs	1 teaspoon garlic powder
1 tablespoon water	¼ teaspoon cayenne pepper
½ cup powdered Parmesan cheese (about 1½ ounces) (or pork dust for dairy-free)	¼ teaspoon fine sea salt
	¼ teaspoon ground black pepper
For Garnish (optional):	
Fresh parsley leaves	Powdered Parmesan cheese
For Serving (optional):	
Prepared yellow mustard	Reduced-sugar or sugar-free ketchup
Ranch Dressing	

1. Spray the Crisper Tray with avocado oil. 2. Using a sharp knife, cut the top ½ inch off the onion and peel off the outer layer. Cut the onion into 8 equal sections, stopping 1 inch from the bottom—you want the onion to stay together at the base. Gently spread the sections, or "petals," apart. 3. Crack the eggs into a large bowl, add the water, and whisk well. Place the onion in the dish and coat it well in the egg. Use a spoon to coat the inside of the onion and all of the petals. 4. In a small bowl, combine the Parmesan, seasonings, salt, and pepper. 5. Place the onion in a casserole dish. Sprinkle the seasoning mixture all over the onion and use your fingers to press it into the petals. Spray the onion with avocado oil. 6. Loosely cover the onion with parchment paper and then foil. Slide the Wire Rack into shelf position 6. Place the casserole dish on the Wire Rack. Select the Bake setting. Set the cooking temperature to 350°F and the cooking time to 30 minutes. Press Start/Pause to begin cooking. Then remove it from the air fryer and increase the air fryer temperature to 400°F. 7. Remove the foil and parchment and spray the onion with avocado oil again. Protecting your hands with oven-safe gloves or a tea towel, transfer the onion to the air fryer. Cook for an additional 3 to 5 minutes, until light brown and crispy. 8. Garnish with fresh parsley and powdered Parmesan, if desired. Serve with mustard, ranch dressing, and ketchup, if desired. 9. Store leftovers in an airtight container in the fridge for up to 4 days. Reheat in a preheated 400°F air fryer for 3 to 5 minutes, until warm and crispy.

Crunchy Calamari Rings

Prep Time: 10 minutes | Cook Time: 15 minutes | Serves: 4

2 large egg yolks	½ teaspoon onion powder
1 cup powdered Parmesan cheese (or pork dust for dairy-free)	1 pound calamari, sliced into rings
¼ cup coconut flour	Fresh oregano leaves, for garnish (optional)
3 teaspoons dried oregano leaves	1 cup marinara sauce, for serving (optional)
½ teaspoon garlic powder	Lemon slices, for serving (optional)

1. Spray the Crisper Tray with avocado oil. 2. In a shallow dish, whisk the egg yolks. In a separate bowl, mix together the Parmesan, coconut flour, and spices. 3. Dip the calamari rings in the egg yolks, tap off any excess egg, then dip them into the cheese mixture and coat well. Use your hands to press the coating onto the calamari if necessary. Spray the coated rings with avocado oil. 4. Place the calamari rings in the Crisper Tray, leaving space between them. Slide the Crisper Tray into shelf position 4/5. Select the Air Fry setting. Set the cooking temperature to 400°F and the cooking time to 15 minutes. Press Start/Pause to begin cooking. Garnish with the fresh oregano, if desired, and serve with marinara sauce for dipping and lemon slices, if desired. 5. Best served fresh. Store leftovers in an airtight container in the fridge for up to 5 days. Reheat in a preheated 400°F air fryer for 3 minutes, or until heated through.

Prosciutto–Wrapped Onion Rings with Guacamole

Prep Time: 10 minutes | Cook Time: 6 minutes | Serves: 4

2 small onions (about 1½ inches in diameter), cut into ½-inch-thick slices	8 slices prosciutto
Guacamole:	
2 avocados, halved, pitted, and peeled	2 small cloves garlic, smashed to a paste
3 tablespoons lime juice, plus more to taste	3 tablespoons chopped fresh cilantro leaves
2 small plum tomatoes, diced	½ scant teaspoon fine sea salt
½ cup finely diced onions	½ scant teaspoon ground cumin

1. Make the guacamole: Place the avocados and lime juice in a large bowl and mash with a fork until it reaches your desired consistency. Add the tomatoes, onions, garlic, cilantro, salt, and cumin and stir until well combined. Taste and add more lime juice if desired. Set aside half of the guacamole for serving. (Note: If you're making the guacamole ahead of time, place it in a large resealable plastic bag, squeeze out all the air, and seal it shut. It will keep in the refrigerator for up to 3 days when stored this way.) 2. Place a piece of parchment paper on a tray that fits in your freezer and place the onion slices on it, breaking the slices apart into 8 rings. Fill each ring with about 2 tablespoons of guacamole. Place the tray in the freezer for 2 hours. 3. Spray the Crisper Tray with avocado oil. 4. Remove the rings from the freezer and wrap each in a slice of prosciutto. Place them in the Crisper Tray, leaving space between them. 5. Slide the Crisper Tray into shelf position 4/5. Select the Air Fry setting. Set the cooking temperature to 400°F and the cooking time to 6 minutes. Press Start/Pause to begin cooking. Flip them halfway through the cooking time. 6. Use a spatula to remove the rings from the air fryer. Serve with the reserved half of the guacamole. 7. Store leftovers in an airtight container in the refrigerator for up to 4 days. Reheat in a preheated 400°F air fryer for about 3 minutes, until heated through.

Cheese Flatbread

Prep Time: 5 minutes | Cook Time: 8 minutes | Serves: 6

1 cup shredded mozzarella cheese	½ cup blanched finely ground almond flour
1-ounce cream cheese, broken into small pieces	

1. Place mozzarella into a large microwave-safe bowl. Add cream cheese pieces. Microwave on high 60 seconds, then stir to combine. Add flour and stir until a soft ball of dough forms. 2. Cut dough ball into two equal pieces. Cut a piece of parchment to fit into the Baking Pan. Press each dough piece into a 5" round on ungreased parchment. 3. Slide the Baking Pan into shelf position 4/5. Select the Bake setting. Set the cooking temperature to 350°F and the cooking time to 8 minutes. Press Start/Pause to begin cooking. Carefully flip the flatbread over halfway through cooking. Flatbread will be golden brown when done. 4. Let flatbread cool 5 minutes, then slice each round into six triangles. Serve warm.

Delicious Prosciutto Pierogi

Prep Time: 15 minutes | Cook Time: 20 minutes | Serves: 4

1 cup chopped cauliflower
2 tablespoons diced onions
1 tablespoon unsalted butter (or lard or bacon fat for dairy-free), melted
Pinch of fine sea salt

½ cup shredded sharp cheddar cheese (about 2 ounces) (or Kite Hill brand cream cheese style spread, softened, for dairy-free)
8 slices prosciutto
Fresh oregano leaves, for garnish (optional)

1. Lightly grease a 7-inch pie pan that will fit in your air fryer. 2. Make the filling: Place the cauliflower and onion in the pan. Drizzle with the melted butter and sprinkle with the salt. Using your hands, mix everything together, making sure the cauliflower is coated in the butter. 3. Slide the wire rack into shelf position 4/5. Place the pan on the wire rack. Select the Bake. Set the temperature to 350°F and the time to 10 minutes. Press Start/Pause to begin cooking. Bake until fork-tender, stirring halfway through. 4. Transfer the cauliflower mixture to a food processor or high-powered blender. Spray the Crisper Tray with avocado oil and increase the air fryer temperature to 400°F. 5. Pulse the cauliflower mixture in the food processor until smooth. Stir in the cheese. 6. Assemble the pierogi: Lay 1 slice of prosciutto on a sheet of parchment paper with a short end toward you. Lay another slice of prosciutto on top of it at a right angle, forming a cross. Spoon about 2 heaping tablespoons of the filling into the center of the cross. 7. Fold each arm of the prosciutto cross over the filling to form a square, making sure that the filling is well covered. Press around the filling with your fingers to make a square shape. Repeat with remaining prosciutto and filling. 8. Spray the pierogi with avocado oil and place them in the Crisper Tray. Slide the Crisper Tray into shelf position 4/5. Select the Air Fry setting. Set the cooking temperature to 350°F and the cooking time to 10 minutes. Press Start/Pause to begin cooking. 9. Garnish with oregano before serving, if desired. Store leftovers in an airtight container in the fridge for up to 4 days. Reheat in a preheated 400°F air fryer for 3 minutes, or until heated through.

Roasted Lime Salsa

Prep Time: 5 minutes | Cook Time: 30 minutes | Serves: 10

2 large San Marzano tomatoes, cored and cut into large chunks
½ medium white onion, peeled and large-diced
½ medium jalapeño, seeded and large-diced
2 cloves garlic, peeled and diced

½ teaspoon salt
1 tablespoon coconut oil
¼ cup fresh lime juice

1. Place tomatoes, onion, and jalapeño into an ungreased 6" round nonstick baking dish. Add garlic, then sprinkle with salt and drizzle with coconut oil. 2. Slide the wire rack into shelf position 4/5. Place the baking dish on the wire rack. Select the Bake. Set the temperature to 300°F and the time to 30 minutes. Press Start/Pause to begin cooking. Vegetables will be dark brown around the edges and tender when done. 3. Pour mixture into a food processor or blender. Add lime juice. Process on low speed 30 seconds until only a few chunks remain. 4. Transfer salsa to a sealable container and refrigerate at least 1 hour. Serve chilled.

Homemade Crispy Deviled Eggs

Prep Time: 10 minutes | Cook Time: 25 minutes | Serves: 6

7 large eggs, divided
1-ounce plain pork rinds, finely crushed
2 tablespoons mayonnaise

¼ teaspoon salt
¼ teaspoon ground black pepper

1. Place 6 whole eggs into ungreased Crisper Tray. Slide the Crisper Tray into shelf position 4/5. Select the Eggs setting. Set the cooking temperature to 220°F and the cooking time to 20 minutes. Press Start/Pause to begin cooking. When done, place eggs into a bowl of ice water to cool 5 minutes. 2. Peel cool eggs, then cut in half lengthwise. Remove yolks and place aside in a medium bowl. 3. In a separate small bowl, whisk remaining raw egg. Place pork rinds in a separate medium bowl. Dip each egg white into whisked egg, then gently coat with pork rinds. Spritz with cooking spray and place into the Crisper Tray. Slide the Crisper Tray into shelf position 4/5. Select the Air Fry setting. Set the cooking temperature to 400°F and the cooking time to 5 minutes. Press Start/Pause to begin cooking, turning eggs halfway through cooking. Eggs will be golden when done. 4. Mash yolks in bowl with mayonnaise until smooth. Sprinkle with salt and pepper and mix. 5. Spoon 2 tablespoons yolk mixture into each fried egg white. Serve warm.

Crispy Bacon–Wrapped Cabbage Bites

Prep Time: 10 minutes | Cook Time: 12 minutes | Serves: 6

3 tablespoons sriracha hot chili sauce, divided
1 medium head cabbage, cored and cut into 12 bite-sized pieces
2 tablespoons coconut oil, melted
½ teaspoon salt

12 slices sugar-free bacon
½ cup mayonnaise
¼ teaspoon garlic powder

1. Evenly brush 2 tablespoons sriracha onto cabbage pieces. Drizzle evenly with coconut oil, then sprinkle with salt. 2. Wrap each cabbage piece with bacon and secure with a toothpick. Place into the Crisper Tray. Slide the Crisper Tray into shelf position 4/5. Select the Air Fry setting. Set the cooking temperature to 375°F and the cooking time to 12 minutes. Press Start/Pause to begin cooking, turning cabbage halfway through cooking. Bacon will be cooked and crispy when done. 3. In a small bowl, whisk together garlic powder, mayonnaise, and remaining sriracha. Use as a dipping sauce for cabbage bites.

Savory Bacon–Cauliflower Skewers

Prep Time: 10 minutes | Cook Time: 12 minutes | Serves: 4

4 slices sugar-free bacon, cut into thirds
¼ medium yellow onion, peeled and cut into 1" pieces
4 ounces (about 8) cauliflower florets

1½ tablespoons olive oil
¼ teaspoon salt
¼ teaspoon garlic powder

1. Place 1 piece of bacon and 2 pieces onion on a 6" skewer. Add a second piece bacon, and 2 cauliflower florets, followed by another piece of bacon onto skewer. Repeat with remaining ingredients and three additional skewers to make four total skewers. 2. Drizzle skewers with olive oil, then sprinkle with salt and garlic powder. Place skewers into the Crisper Tray. Slide the Crisper Tray into shelf position 4/5. Select the Air Fry setting. Set the cooking temperature to 375°F and the cooking time to 12 minutes. Press Start/Pause to begin cooking, turning the skewers halfway through cooking. 3. When done, vegetables will be tender and bacon will be crispy. Serve warm.

Pork Sausage–Stuffed Mushrooms

Prep Time: 10 minutes | Cook Time: 20 minutes | Serves: 6

½ pound ground pork sausage
¼ teaspoon salt
¼ teaspoon garlic powder

2 medium scallions, trimmed and chopped
½ ounce plain pork rinds, finely crushed
1 pound cremini mushrooms, stems removed

1. In a large bowl, mix sausage, salt, garlic powder, scallions, and pork rinds. Scoop 1 tablespoon mixture into center of each mushroom cap. 2. Place mushrooms into the Crisper Tray. Slide the Crisper Tray into shelf position 4/5. Select the Air Fry setting. Set the cooking temperature to 375°F and the cooking time to 20 minutes. Press Start/Pause to begin cooking. Pork will be fully cooked to at least 145°F in the center and browned when done. Serve warm.

Crispy Avocado Fries

Prep Time: 10 minutes | Cook Time: 6 minutes | Serves: 6

1 large egg
¼ cup coconut flour

2 ounces plain pork rinds, finely crushed
2 medium avocados, peeled, pitted, and sliced into ¼"-thick fries

1. Whisk egg in a medium bowl. Place coconut flour and pork rinds in two separate medium bowls. 2. Dip 1 avocado slice into egg, then coat in coconut flour. Dip in egg once more, then press gently into pork rinds to coat on both sides. Repeat with remaining avocado slices. 3. Place slices into the Crisper Tray. Slide the Crisper Tray into shelf position 4/5. Select the Air Fry setting. Set the cooking temperature to 400°F and the cooking time to 6 minutes. Press Start/Pause to begin cooking, turning "fries" halfway through. Fries will be crispy on the outside and soft inside when done. Let cool before serving.

Hot & Spicy Turkey Meatballs

Prep Time: 10 minutes | Cook Time: 15 minutes | Serves: 4

1 pound 85/15 ground turkey	½ teaspoon salt
1 large egg, whisked	½ teaspoon paprika
¼ cup sriracha hot chili sauce	¼ teaspoon ground black pepper

1. Combine all ingredients in a large bowl. Roll mixture into eighteen meatballs, about 3 tablespoons each. 2. Place meatballs into the Crisper Tray. Slide the Crisper Tray into shelf position 4/5. Select the Air Fry setting. Set the cooking temperature to 375°F and the cooking time to 15 minutes. Press Start/Pause to begin cooking, shaking the tray three times during cooking. 3. Meatballs will be done when browned and internal temperature is at least 165°F. Serve warm.

Salami Cream Cheese Roll-Ups

Prep Time: 5 minutes | Cook Time: 4 minutes | Serves: 4

4 ounces cream cheese, broken into 16 equal pieces	16 (0.5-ounce) deli slices Genoa salami

1. Place a piece of cream cheese at the edge of a slice of salami and roll to close. Secure with a toothpick. Repeat with remaining cream cheese pieces and salami. 2. Place roll-ups in an ungreased 6" round nonstick baking dish. Slide the wire rack into shelf position 4/5. Place the baking dish on the wire rack. Select the Bake. Set the temperature to 350°F and the time to 4 minutes. Press Start/Pause to begin cooking. 3. Salami will be crispy and cream cheese will be warm when done. Let cool 5 minutes before serving.

Crispy Parmesan Zucchini Fries

Prep Time: 2 hours 10 minutes | Cook Time: 10 minutes | Serves: 8

2 medium zucchini, ends removed, quartered lengthwise, and sliced into 3"-long fries	½ cup blanched finely ground almond flour
½ teaspoon salt	¾ cup grated Parmesan cheese
⅓ cup heavy whipping cream	1 teaspoon Italian seasoning

1. Sprinkle the zucchini with salt and wrap in a kitchen towel to draw out excess moisture. Let sit 2 hours. 2. Pour cream into a medium bowl. In a separate medium bowl, whisk together flour, Parmesan, and Italian seasoning. 3. Place each zucchini fry into cream, then gently shake off excess. Press each fry into dry mixture, coating each side, then place into the Crisper Tray. Slide the Crisper Tray into shelf position 4/5. Select the Air Fry setting. Set the cooking temperature to 400°F and the cooking time to 10 minutes. Press Start/Pause to begin cooking, turning fries halfway through cooking. Fries will be golden and crispy when done. 4. Place on clean parchment sheet to cool 5 minutes before serving.

Fried Ranch Parmesan Pickles

Prep Time: 40 minutes | Cook Time: 10 minutes | Serves: 4

4 dill pickle spears, halved lengthwise	½ cup grated Parmesan cheese
¼ cup ranch dressing	2 tablespoons dry ranch seasoning
½ cup blanched finely ground almond flour	

1. Wrap spears in a kitchen towel 30 minutes to soak up excess pickle juice. 2. Pour ranch dressing into a medium bowl and add pickle spears. In a separate medium bowl, mix flour, Parmesan, and ranch seasoning. 3. Remove each spear from ranch dressing and shake off excess. Press gently into dry mixture to coat all sides. 4. Place spears into the Crisper Tray. Slide the Crisper Tray into shelf position 4/5. Select the Air Fry setting. Set the cooking temperature to 400°F and the cooking time to 10 minutes. Press Start/Pause to begin cooking, turning spears three times during cooking. Serve warm.

Crunchy Bacon–Wrapped Mozzarella Sticks

Prep Time: 12 minutes | Cook Time: 12 minutes | Serves: 6

6 sticks mozzarella string cheese	6 slices sugar-free bacon

1. Place mozzarella sticks on a medium plate, cover, and place into freezer 1 hour until frozen solid. 2. Wrap each mozzarella stick in 1 piece of bacon and secure with a toothpick. Place into the Crisper Tray. Slide the Crisper Tray into shelf position 4/5. Select the Air Fry setting. Set the cooking temperature to 400°F and the cooking time to 12 minutes. Press Start/Pause to begin cooking, turning sticks once during cooking. Bacon will be crispy when done. 3. Serve warm.

Tasty Buffalo Cauliflower Bites

Prep Time: 5 minutes | Cook Time: 15 minutes | Serves: 6

1 medium head cauliflower, leaves and core removed, cut into bite-sized pieces 4 tablespoons salted butter, melted	¼ cup dry ranch seasoning ⅓ cup buffalo sauce

1. Place cauliflower pieces into a large bowl. Pour butter over cauliflower and toss to coat. Sprinkle in ranch seasoning and toss to coat. 2. Place cauliflower into the Crisper Tray. Slide the Crisper Tray into shelf position 4/5. Select the Air Fry setting. Set the cooking temperature to 350°F and the cooking time to 12 minutes. Press Start/Pause to begin cooking, shaking the tray three times during cooking. 3. When timer beeps, place cooked cauliflower in a clean large bowl. Toss with buffalo sauce, then return to the air fryer to cook another 3 minutes. Cauliflower bites will be darkened at the edges and tender when done. Serve warm.

Crispy Ranch Kale Chips

Prep Time: 5 minutes | Cook Time: 10 minutes | Serves: 8

½ teaspoon dried chives ½ teaspoon dried dill weed ½ teaspoon dried parsley ¼ teaspoon garlic powder	¼ teaspoon onion powder ⅛ teaspoon fine sea salt ⅛ teaspoon ground black pepper 2 large bunches kale

1. Spray the Crisper Tray with avocado oil. 2. Place the seasonings, salt, and pepper in a small bowl and mix well. 3. Wash the kale and pat completely dry. Use a sharp knife to carve out the thick inner stems, then spray the leaves with avocado oil and sprinkle them with the seasoning mix. 4. Place the kale leaves on the Crisper Tray in a single layer and slide the Crisper Tray into shelf position 4/5. Select the Fries setting. Set the cooking temperature to 360°F/182°C and the cooking time to 10 minutes. 5. Shake and rotate the chips halfway through. Transfer the cooked chips to a baking sheet to cool completely and crisp up. Repeat with the remaining kale. Sprinkle the cooled chips with salt before serving, if desired. 6. Kale chips can be stored in an airtight container at room temperature for up to 1 week, but they are best eaten within 3 days.

Crispy Onion Rings

Prep Time: 10 minutes | Cook Time: 5 minutes | Serves: 8

1 large egg ¼ cup coconut flour	2 ounces plain pork rinds, finely crushed 1 large white onion, peeled and sliced into 8 (¼") rings

1. Whisk egg in a medium bowl. Place coconut flour and pork rinds in two separate medium bowls. Dip each onion ring into egg, then coat in coconut flour. Dip coated onion ring in egg once more, then press gently into pork rinds to cover all sides. 2. Place rings into ungreased Crisper Tray. Slide the Crisper Tray into shelf position 4/5. Select the Air Fry setting. Set the cooking temperature to 400°F and the cooking time to 5 minutes. Press Start/Pause to begin cooking. Flip them halfway through the cooking time. 3. Onion rings will be golden and crispy when done. Serve warm.

Spicy Nacho Avocado Fries

Prep Time: 10 minutes | Cook Time: 15 minutes | Serves: 6

3 firm, barely ripe avocados, halved, peeled, and pitted
2 cups pork dust (or powdered Parmesan cheese for vegetarian)
2 teaspoons fine sea salt
2 teaspoons ground black pepper
2 teaspoons ground cumin
1 teaspoon chili powder

1 teaspoon paprika
½ teaspoon garlic powder
½ teaspoon onion powder
2 large eggs
Salsa, for serving (optional)
Fresh chopped cilantro leaves, for garnish (optional)

1. Spray the Crisper Tray with avocado oil. 2. Slice the avocados into thick-cut french fry shapes. 3. In a bowl, mix together the salt, pork dust, pepper, and seasonings. 4. In a separate shallow bowl, whip the eggs. 5. Dip the avocado fries into the beaten eggs, shaking off any excess, and dip them into the pork dust mixture. Use your hands to press the breading into each fry. 6. Spray the fries with avocado oil and place them on the Crisper Tray in a single layer, leaving space between them. If there are too many fries to fit in a single layer, work in batches. 7. Slide the Tray into shelf position 4/5. Select the Fries setting. Set the cooking temperature to 400°F/204°C and the cooking time to 13 minutes. Cook for 13 to 15 minutes, until golden brown, flipping after 5 minutes. 8. Serve with the salsa, if desired, and garnish with the fresh chopped cilantro, if desired. Best served fresh. 9. Store leftovers in an airtight container in the fridge for up to 5 days. Reheat in the Air Fryer at 400°F/204°C for 3 minutes until heated through.

Hot Cauliflower with Blue Cheese Dressing

Prep Time: 5 minutes | Cook Time: 11 minutes | Serves: 4

¼ cup hot sauce
¼ cup powdered Parmesan cheese
Blue Cheese Dressing, for serving:
8 ounces crumbled blue cheese, plus more if desired for a chunky texture
¼ cup beef bone broth
¼ cup full-fat sour cream
¼ cup red wine vinegar or coconut vinegar

2 tablespoons unsalted butter, melted
1 small head cauliflower, cut into 1-inch bites

1½ tablespoons Swerve confectioners'-style sweetener or equivalent amount of liquid or powdered sweetener
1 tablespoon MCT oil
1 clove garlic, peeled

1. Spray a baking dish that fits in the appliance with avocado oil. 2. Place the hot sauce, Parmesan, and butter in a large bowl and stir to well-combined. Add the cauliflower and toss to coat well. 3. Place the coated cauliflower in the baking dish. Slide the Crisper Tray with the dish on top into shelf position 4/5. 4. Select the Vegetables setting. Set the cooking temperature to 400°F/204°C and the cooking time to 11 minutes. Stir halfway through. Serve with blue cheese dressing. 5. Make blue cheese dressing by placing all the ingredients in a food processor and blend them until smooth. Transfer to a jar. Stir in extra chunks of blue cheese if desired. There will be about 2 cups. Store in the refrigerator for up to 5 days. 6. Store leftovers in an airtight container in the fridge for up to 4 days. Reheat in the Air Fryer at 400°F/204°C for 3 minutes, until warmed through and crispy.

Crispy Bacon–Wrapped Pickle Poppers

Prep Time: 10 minutes | Cook Time: 10 minutes | Serves: 4

12 medium dill pickles
1 (8-ounce) package cream cheese, softened
1 cup shredded sharp cheddar cheese (about 4 ounces)

12 slices bacon or beef bacon, sliced in half lengthwise
Ranch Dressing or Blue Cheese Dressing for serving (optional)

1. Spray the Baking Pan with avocado oil. 2. Slice the dill pickles in half lengthwise and use a spoon to scoop out the centers. 3. Place the cream cheese and cheddar cheese in a small bowl and stir until well combined. 4. Divide the cream cheese mixture among the pickles, spooning equal amounts into the scooped-out centers. Wrap each filled pickle with a slice of bacon and secure the bacon with toothpicks. 5. Place the bacon-wrapped pickles on the Baking Pan with the bacon seam side down and slide the Pan into shelf position 4/5. Select the Bacon setting. Set the cooking temperature to 400°F/204°C and the cooking time to 8 minutes. Cook for 8 to 10 minutes, until the bacon is crispy, flipping halfway through. Serve warm with the ranch or blue cheese dressing, if desired. 6. Best served fresh. Store leftovers in an airtight container in the fridge for up to 5 days. Reheat in the Air Fryer at 400°F/204°C for 3 minutes, or until heated through.

Chapter 4 Poultry

Savory Garlic Parmesan Drumsticks

Prep Time: 5 minutes | Cook Time: 25 minutes | Serves: 4

8 (4-ounce) chicken drumsticks	2 tablespoons salted butter, melted
½ teaspoon salt	½ cup grated Parmesan cheese
⅛ teaspoon ground black pepper	1 tablespoon dried parsley
½ teaspoon garlic powder	

1. Sprinkle drumsticks with pepper, salt, and garlic powder. Place drumsticks on the Crisper Tray and slide the Tray into shelf position 4/5. 2. Select the Chicken setting. Set the cooking temperature to 400°F/204°C and the cooking time to 25 minutes. 3. Turn drumsticks halfway through cooking. Drumsticks will be golden and have an internal temperature of at least 165°F when done. 4. Transfer drumsticks to a large serving dish. Pour butter over drumsticks, and sprinkle with Parmesan and parsley. Serve warm.

Simple Pecan–Crusted Chicken Tenders

Prep Time: 10 minutes | Cook Time: 12 minutes | Serves: 4

2 tablespoons mayonnaise	½ teaspoon salt
1 teaspoon Dijon mustard	¼ teaspoon ground black pepper
1 pound boneless, skinless chicken tenders	½ cup chopped roasted pecans, finely ground

1. In a small bowl, whisk mayonnaise and mustard until combined. Brush mixture onto chicken tenders on both sides and sprinkle tenders with pepper and salt. 2. Place pecans in a medium bowl and press each tender into pecans to coat each side. 3. Place tenders on the Crisper Tray in a single layer, working in batches if needed, and slide the Tray into shelf position 4/5. Select the Chicken setting. Set the cooking temperature to 375°F/190°C and the cooking time to 12 minutes. 4. Turn tenders halfway through cooking. Tenders will be golden brown and have an internal temperature of at least 165°F when done. Serve warm.

Traditional General Tso's Chicken

Prep Time: 10 minutes | Cook Time: 20 minutes | Serves: 4

1 pound boneless, skinless chicken breasts or thighs, cut into 1-inch cubes	Fine sea salt and ground black pepper
General Tso's Sauce:	
½ cup chicken broth	aminos
⅓ cup Swerve confectioners'-style sweetener or equivalent amount of liquid or powdered sweetener	3 small dried red chiles, chopped
¼ cup coconut vinegar or unseasoned rice vinegar	1 clove garlic, minced
¼ cup thinly sliced green onions, plus more for garnish if desired	1½ teaspoons grated fresh ginger
1 tablespoon plus 1¼ teaspoons wheat-free tamari, or ¼ cup coconut	1 teaspoon toasted sesame oil
	¼ teaspoon guar gum (optional)
For Serving (optional):	
Fried Cauliflower Rice	Sautéed broccoli rabe
For Garnish (optional):	
Diced red chiles	Sesame seeds
Red pepper flakes	

1. Very lightly season the chicken on all sides with salt and pepper (the sauce will add seasoning). Place the chicken in a single layer in the Baking Pan. Slide the Baking Pan into shelf position 4/5. Select the Chicken setting. Set the cooking temperature to 400°F and the cooking time to 5 minutes. Press Start/Pause to begin cooking. 2. While the chicken cooks, make the sauce: In a small bowl, stir together all the sauce ingredients except the guar gum until well combined. Sift in the guar gum (if using) and whisk until well combined. 3. Pour the sauce over the chicken and, stirring every 5 minutes, cook for another 12 to 15 minutes, until the sauce is bubbly and thick and the chicken is cooked through and the internal temperature reaches 165°F. 4. If you want the sauce to be even thicker and more flavorful, remove the chicken and return the sauce to the air fryer to cook for 5 to 10 minutes longer. 5. Transfer the chicken to a large bowl. Serve with fried cauliflower rice and sautéed broccoli rabe, if desired, and garnish with diced red chiles, sliced green onions, red pepper flakes, and sesame seeds, if desired. 6. Store leftovers in an airtight container in the refrigerator for up to 4 days. Reheat in a preheated 375°F air fryer for 5 minutes, or until heated through.

Chili Fajita–Stuffed Chicken Breast

Prep Time: 15 minutes | Cook Time: 25 minutes | Serves: 4

2 (6-ounce) boneless, skinless chicken breasts
¼ medium white onion, peeled and sliced
1 medium green bell pepper, seeded and sliced
1 tablespoon coconut oil

2 teaspoons chili powder
1 teaspoon ground cumin
½ teaspoon garlic powder

1. Slice each chicken breast completely in half lengthwise into two even pieces. Using a meat tenderizer, pound out the chicken until it's about ¼" thickness. 2. Lay each slice of chicken out and place three slices of onion and four slices of green pepper on the end closest to you. Begin rolling the peppers and onions tightly into the chicken. Secure the roll with either toothpicks or a couple pieces of butcher's twine. 3. Drizzle coconut oil over chicken. Sprinkle each side with chili powder, cumin, and garlic powder. Place each roll on the Crisper Tray and slide the Tray into shelf position 4/5. 4. Select the Chicken setting. Set the cooking temperature to 350°F/177°C and the cooking time to 25 minutes. 5. Serve warm.

Parmesan Chicken with Lemon Butter Sauce

Prep Time: 10 minutes | Cook Time: 10 minutes | Serves: 2

2 large eggs, room temperature
1 tablespoon water
½ cup powdered Parmesan cheese (about 1½ ounces) or pork dust
2 teaspoons dried thyme leaves
Lemon Butter Sauce:

1 teaspoon ground black pepper
2 (5-ounce) boneless, skinless chicken breasts, pounded to ½ inch thick

2 tablespoons unsalted butter, melted
2 teaspoons lemon juice
¼ teaspoon finely chopped fresh thyme leaves, plus more for garnish

⅛ teaspoon fine sea salt
Lemon slices, for serving

1. Spray the Crisper Tray with avocado oil. 2. Beat the eggs in a shallow bowl, then add the water and stir well. 3. In a separate shallow bowl, mix together the Parmesan, thyme, and pepper until well combined. 4. One at a time, dip the chicken breasts in the eggs and let any excess drip off, then dredge both sides of the chicken in the Parmesan mixture. As you finish, set the coated chicken in the Crisper Tray. 5. Slide the Crisper Tray into shelf position 4/5. Select the Chicken setting. Set the cooking temperature to 390°F and the cooking time to 10 minutes. Press Start/Pause to begin cooking. Flip them halfway through the cooking time. Cook until cooked through and the internal temperature reaches 165°F. 6. While the chicken cooks, make the lemon butter sauce: In a small bowl, mix together all the sauce ingredients until well combined. 7. Plate the chicken and pour the sauce over it. Garnish with chopped fresh thyme and serve with lemon slices. 8. Store leftovers in an airtight container in the refrigerator for up to 4 days. Reheat in a preheated 390°F air fryer for 5 minutes, or until heated through.

Bacon–Wrapped Chicken Pockets

Prep Time: 10 minutes | Cook Time: 20 minutes | Serves: 4

4 (5-ounce) boneless, skinless chicken breasts, pounded to ¼ inch thick
2 (5.2-ounce) packages Boursin cheese (or Kite Hill brand chive

cream cheese style spread, softened, for dairy-free)
8 slices thin-cut bacon or beef bacon
Sprig of fresh cilantro, for garnish (optional)

1. Spray the Crisper Tray with avocado oil. 2. Place one of the chicken breasts on a cutting board. With a sharp knife held parallel to the cutting board, make a 1-inch-wide incision at the top of the breast. Carefully cut into the breast to form a large pocket, leaving a ½-inch border along the sides and bottom. Repeat with the other 3 chicken breasts. 3. Snip the corner of a large resealable plastic bag to form a ¾-inch hole. Place the Boursin cheese in the bag and pipe the cheese into the pockets in the chicken breasts, dividing the cheese evenly among them. 4. Wrap 2 slices of bacon around each chicken breast and secure the ends with toothpicks. Place the bacon-wrapped chicken in the Crisper Tray. 5. Slide the Crisper Tray into shelf position 4/5. Select the Air Fry setting. Set the cooking temperature to 400°F and the cooking time to 20 minutes. Press Start/Pause to begin cooking. Flip them halfway through the cooking time. Garnish with a sprig of cilantro before serving, if desired. 6. Store leftovers in an airtight container in the refrigerator for up to 4 days. Reheat in a preheated 400°F air fryer for 5 minutes, or until warmed through.

Italian Chicken Parmesan

Prep Time: 10 minutes | Cook Time: 25 minutes | Serves: 4

2 (6-ounce) boneless, skinless chicken breasts
½ teaspoon garlic powder
¼ teaspoon dried oregano
½ teaspoon dried parsley
4 tablespoons full-fat mayonnaise, divided

1 cup shredded mozzarella cheese, divided
1 ounce pork rinds, crushed
½ cup grated Parmesan cheese, divided
1 cup low-carb, no-sugar-added pasta sauce

1. Cut each chicken breast in half lengthwise and pound out to ¾" thickness. Sprinkle with oregano, garlic powder, and parsley. 2. Spread 1 tablespoon mayonnaise on top of each piece of chicken and sprinkle ¼ cup mozzarella on each piece. 3. In a small bowl, mix the crushed pork rinds and Parmesan. Sprinkle the mixture on top of mozzarella. 4. Pour sauce into 6" round baking pan that fits in the appliance and place chicken on top. Slide the Crisper Tray with the pan on top into shelf position 4/5. 5. Select the Chicken setting. Set the cooking temperature to 320°F/160°C and the cooking time to 25 minutes. 6. Cheese will be browned and internal temperature of the chicken will be at least 165°F when fully cooked. Serve warm.

Creamy Chicken Cordon Bleu Casserole

Prep Time: 15 minutes | Cook Time: 15 minutes | Serves: 4

2 cups cubed cooked chicken thigh meat
½ cup cubed cooked ham
2 ounces Swiss cheese, cubed
4 ounces full-fat cream cheese, softened

1 tablespoon heavy cream
2 tablespoons unsalted butter, melted
2 teaspoons Dijon mustard
1 ounce pork rinds, crushed

1. Place chicken and ham into a 6" round baking pan that fits in the appliance and toss so meat is evenly mixed. Sprinkle cheese cubes on top of meat. 2. In a large bowl, mix cream cheese, heavy cream, butter, and mustard and then pour the mixture over the meat and cheese. Top with pork rinds. Slide the Crisper Tray with the pan on top into shelf position 4/5. 3. Select the Chicken setting. Set the cooking temperature to 350°F/177°C and the cooking time to 15 minutes. 4. The casserole will be browned and bubbling when done. Serve warm.

Paprika Chicken Strips with Satay Sauce

Prep Time: 5 minutes | Cook Time: 10 minutes | Serves: 4

4 (6-ounce) boneless, skinless chicken breasts, sliced into 16 (1-inch) strips
Sauce:
¼ cup creamy almond butter (or sunflower seed butter for nut-free)
2 tablespoons chicken broth
1½ tablespoons coconut vinegar or unseasoned rice vinegar
1 clove garlic, minced
For Garnish/Serving (optional):
¼ cup chopped cilantro leaves
Red pepper flakes
Special Equipment:
16 wooden or bamboo skewers, soaked in water for 15 minutes

1 teaspoon fine sea salt
1 teaspoon paprika

1 teaspoon peeled and minced fresh ginger
½ teaspoon hot sauce
⅛ teaspoon stevia glycerite, or 2 to 3 drops liquid stevia

Sea salt flakes
Thinly sliced orange, red, and yellow bell peppers

1. Spray the Crisper Tray with avocado oil. 2. Thread the chicken strips onto the skewers. Season on all sides with the salt and paprika. Place the chicken skewers in the Crisper Tray. Slide the Crisper Tray into shelf position 4/5. Select the Air Fry setting. Set the cooking temperature to 400°F and the cooking time to 10 minutes. Press Start/Pause to begin cooking. Flip them halfway through the cooking time. Cook until the chicken is cooked through and the internal temperature reaches 165°F. 3. While the chicken skewers cook, make the sauce: In a medium-sized bowl, stir together all the sauce ingredients until well combined. Taste and adjust the sweetness and heat to your liking. 4. Garnish the chicken with cilantro, red pepper flakes, and salt flakes, if desired, and serve with sliced bell peppers, if desired. Serve the sauce on the side. 5. Store leftovers in an airtight container in the fridge for up to 4 days or in the freezer for up to a month. Reheat in a preheated 350°F air fryer for 3 minutes per side, or until heated through.

Hearty Jalapeño Popper Hasselback Chicken

Prep Time: 20 minutes | Cook Time: 20 minutes | Serves: 2

4 slices sugar-free bacon, cooked and crumbled
2 ounces full-fat cream cheese, softened
½ cup shredded sharp Cheddar cheese, divided

¼ cup sliced pickled jalapeños
2 (6-ounce) boneless, skinless chicken breasts

1. In a medium bowl, place cooked bacon, then fold in cream cheese, half of the Cheddar, and the jalapeño slices. 2. Use a sharp knife to make slits in each of the chicken breasts about ¾ of the way across the chicken, being careful not to cut all the way through. Depending on the size of the chicken breast, you'll likely have 6–8 slits per breast. 3. Spoon the cream cheese mixture into the slits of the chicken. Sprinkle remaining shredded cheese over chicken breasts and place on the Crisper Tray and slide the Tray into shelf position 4/5. 4. Select the Chicken setting. Set the cooking temperature to 350°F/177°C and the cooking time to 20 minutes. 5. Serve warm.

Delicious Chicken Pesto Parmigiana

Prep Time: 10 minutes | Cook Time: 23 minutes | Serves: 4

2 large eggs
1 tablespoon water
Fine sea salt and ground black pepper
1 cup powdered Parmesan cheese (about 3 ounces)
2 teaspoons Italian seasoning
4 (5-ounce) boneless, skinless chicken breasts or thighs, pounded to

¼ inch thick
1 cup pesto
1 cup shredded mozzarella cheese (about 4 ounces)
Finely chopped fresh basil, for garnish (optional)
Grape tomatoes, halved, for serving (optional)

1. Spray the Crisper Tray with avocado oil. 2. Crack the eggs into a shallow baking dish, add the water and a pinch each of salt and pepper, and whisk to combine. In another shallow baking dish, stir together the Parmesan and Italian seasoning until well combined. 3. Season the chicken breasts well on both sides with salt and pepper. Dip one chicken breast in the eggs and let any excess drip off, then dredge both sides of the breast in the Parmesan mixture. Spray the breast with avocado oil and place it in the Crisper Tray. Repeat with the remaining 3 chicken breasts. 4. Slide the Crisper Tray into shelf position 4/5. Select the Chicken setting. Set the cooking temperature to 400°F and the cooking time to 20 minutes. Press Start/Pause to begin cooking. Cook until the internal temperature reaches 165°F and the breading is golden brown, flipping halfway through. 5. Dollop each chicken breast with ¼ cup of the pesto and top with the mozzarella. Return the breasts to the air fryer and cook for 3 minutes, or until the cheese is melted. Garnish with basil and serve with halved grape tomatoes on the side, if desired. 6. Store leftovers in an airtight container in the refrigerator for up to 4 days. Reheat in a preheated 400°F air fryer for 5 minutes, or until warmed through.

Crispy Spiced Chicken with Cheese

Prep Time: 10 minutes | Cook Time: 23 minutes | Serves: 4

2 large eggs
1 tablespoon water
Fine sea salt and ground black pepper
1 cup pork dust
1 teaspoon ground cumin
1 teaspoon smoked paprika

4 (5-ounce) boneless, skinless chicken breasts or thighs, pounded to
¼ inch thick
1 cup salsa
1 cup shredded Monterey Jack cheese (about 4 ounces) (omit for dairy-free)
Sprig of fresh cilantro, for garnish (optional)

1. Spray the Crisper Tray with avocado oil. 2. Crack the eggs into a shallow bowl, add the water and a pinch each of salt and pepper, and whisk to combine. In another shallow bowl, stir together the pork dust, cumin, and paprika until well combined. 3. Season the chicken breasts well on both sides with salt and pepper. Dip 1 chicken breast in the eggs and let any excess drip off, then dredge both sides of the chicken breast in the pork dust mixture. Spray the breast with avocado oil and place it in the Crisper Tray. Repeat with the remaining 3 chicken breasts. 4. Slide the Crisper Tray into shelf position 4/5. Select the Air Fry setting. Set the cooking temperature to 400°F and the cooking time to 20 minutes. Press Start/Pause to begin cooking. Cook until the internal temperature reaches 165°F and the breading is golden brown, flipping halfway through. 5. Dollop each chicken breast with ¼ cup of the salsa and top with ¼ cup of the cheese. Return the breasts to the air fryer and cook for 3 minutes, or until the cheese is melted. Garnish with cilantro before serving, if desired. 6. Store leftovers in an airtight container in the refrigerator for up to 4 days. Reheat in a preheated 400°F air fryer for 5 minutes, or until warmed through.

Chicken Lettuce Tacos with Lime Peanut Sauce

Prep Time: 10 minutes | Cook Time: 6 minutes | Serves: 4

1-pound ground chicken
¼ cup diced onions (about 1 small onion)
Sauce:
¼ cup creamy peanut butter, room temperature
2 tablespoons chicken broth, plus more if needed
2 tablespoons lime juice
2 tablespoons grated fresh ginger
For Serving:
2 small heads butter lettuce, leaves separated
For Garnish (optional):
Cilantro leaves
Shredded purple cabbage

2 cloves garlic, minced
¼ teaspoon fine sea salt

2 tablespoons wheat-free tamari or coconut aminos
1½ teaspoons hot sauce
5 drops liquid stevia (optional)

Lime slices (optional)

Sliced green onions

1. Place the ground chicken, onions, garlic, and salt in the Baking Pan. Break up the chicken with a spatula. 2. Slide the pan into shelf position 4/5. Select the Bake setting. Set the cooking temperature to 350°F and the cooking time to 5 minutes. Press Start/Pause to begin cooking. Cook until the chicken is browned and cooked through. Break up the chicken again into small crumbles. 3. Make the sauce: In a medium-sized bowl, stir together the peanut butter, broth, lime juice, ginger, tamari, hot sauce, and stevia (if using) until well combined. If the sauce is too thick, add another tablespoon or two of broth. Taste and add more hot sauce if desired. 4. Add half of the sauce to the pan with the chicken. Cook for another minute, until heated through, and stir well to combine. 5. Assemble the tacos: Place several lettuce leaves on a serving plate. Place a few tablespoons of the chicken mixture in each lettuce leaf and garnish with cilantro leaves, purple cabbage, and sliced green onions, if desired. Serve the remaining sauce on the side. Serve with lime slices, if desired. 6. Store leftover meat mixture in an airtight container in the refrigerator for up to 4 days; store leftover sauce, lettuce leaves, and garnishes separately. 7. Reheat the meat mixture in a lightly Baking Pan in a preheated 350°F air fryer for 3 minutes, or until heated through.

Tender Blackened Chicken Tenders

Prep Time: 5 minutes | Cook Time: 12 minutes | Serves: 4

1 pound boneless, skinless chicken tenders
2 tablespoons coconut oil, melted
1 teaspoon paprika
½ teaspoon chili powder

½ teaspoon salt
¼ teaspoon ground black pepper
¼ teaspoon garlic powder
¼ teaspoon cayenne pepper

1. In a large bowl, toss chicken tenders in coconut oil. Sprinkle each side of chicken tenders with paprika, salt, chili powder, black pepper, garlic powder, and cayenne pepper. 2. Place tenders on the Crisper Tray in a single layer and slide the Crisper Tray into shelf position 4/5. Select the Chicken setting. Set the cooking temperature to 375°F/190°C and the cooking time to 12 minutes. 3. Tenders will be dark brown and have an internal temperature of at least 165°F when done. Serve warm.

Chipotle Aioli Chicken Wings

Prep Time: 5 minutes | Cook Time: 25 minutes | Serves: 6

2 pounds bone-in chicken wings
½ teaspoon salt
¼ teaspoon ground black pepper

2 tablespoons mayonnaise
2 teaspoons chipotle powder
2 tablespoons lemon juice

1. In a large bowl, toss the chicken wings in salt and pepper, then place into ungreased Crisper Tray. 2. Slide the Crisper Tray into shelf position 4/5 and slide the Baking Pan into shelf position 6 to catch the drippings. Select the Wings setting. Set the cooking temperature to 400°F and the cooking time to 25 minutes. Press Start/Pause to begin cooking, shaking the tray twice while cooking. Wings will be done when golden and have an internal temperature of at least 165°F. 3 In a small bowl, whisk together the mayonnaise, chipotle powder, and lemon juice. 4. Place cooked wings into a large serving bowl and drizzle with aioli. Toss to coat. Serve warm.

Cheese Chicken Patties

Prep Time: 10 minutes | Cook Time: 10 minutes | Serves: 6

Patties:

1-pound ground chicken
⅓ cup shredded cheddar cheese (omit for dairy-free)
2 tablespoons diced onions, or ¼ teaspoon onion powder

2 tablespoons mayonnaise
1 teaspoon dill pickle juice
1 teaspoon fine sea salt

Coating:

1 cup pork dust

For Serving (optional):

Cornichons
Mayonnaise

Prepared yellow mustard

1. Spray the Crisper Tray with avocado oil. 2. Place the ingredients for the patties in a medium bowl and combine well with your hands. Form the mixture into six 3½-inch patties. 3. Place the pork dust in a shallow bowl. Dredge each patty in the pork dust and use your hands to press the pork dust into a crust around the patty. 4. Working in batches if necessary, place the patties in the Crisper Tray, leaving space between them. 5. Slide the Crisper Tray into shelf position 4/5. Select the Air Fry setting. Set the cooking temperature to 375°F and the cooking time to 10 minutes. Press Start/Pause to begin cooking. Flip them halfway through the cooking time. Cook until the coating is golden brown and the chicken is no longer pink inside. 6. Serve the patties with cornichons, mayo, and mustard, if desired. 7. Store leftovers in an airtight container in the refrigerator for up to 3 days. Reheat in a preheated 350°F air fryer for 4 minutes, or until heated through.

Butter Roasted Whole Chicken with Bacon

Prep Time: 10 minutes | Cook Time: 65 minutes | Serves: 6

1 (4-pound) whole chicken
2 tablespoons salted butter, softened
1 teaspoon dried thyme
½ teaspoon garlic powder

1 teaspoon salt
½ teaspoon ground black pepper
6 slices sugar-free bacon

1. Pat chicken dry with a paper towel, then rub with butter on all sides. Sprinkle thyme, salt, garlic powder, and pepper over chicken. 2. Place chicken into ungreased Crisper Tray, breast side up. Lay strips of bacon over chicken and secure with toothpicks. 3. Slide the Crisper Tray into shelf position 4/5. Select the Chicken setting. Set the cooking temperature to 350°F and the cooking time to 65 minutes. Press Start/Pause to begin cooking. Halfway through cooking, remove and set aside bacon and flip chicken over. 4. Chicken will be done when the skin is golden and crispy and the internal temperature is at least 165°F. Serve warm with bacon.

Traditional Hasselback Alfredo Chicken

Prep Time: 10 minutes | Cook Time: 20 minutes | Serves: 4

4 (6-ounce) boneless, skinless chicken breasts
4 teaspoons coconut oil
½ teaspoon salt
¼ teaspoon ground black pepper

4 strips cooked sugar-free bacon, broken into 24 pieces
½ cup Alfredo sauce
1 cup shredded mozzarella cheese
¼ teaspoon crushed red pepper flakes

1. Cut six horizontal slits in the top of each chicken breast. Drizzle with the coconut oil and sprinkle with black pepper and salt. Place into an ungreased 6" round nonstick baking dish that fits in the appliance. 2. Place 1 bacon piece in each slit in chicken breasts. Pour Alfredo sauce over chicken and sprinkle with mozzarella and red pepper flakes. 3. Slide the Crisper Tray with the dish on top into shelf position 4/5. Select the Chicken setting. Set the cooking temperature to 370°F/187°C and the cooking time to 20 minutes. 4. Chicken will be done when internal temperature is at least 165°F and cheese is browned. Serve warm.

Easy Chicken Cordon Bleu

Prep Time: 15 minutes | Cook Time: 25 minutes | Serves: 4

4 (6-ounce) boneless, skinless chicken breasts	¼ cup Dijon mustard
4 (1-ounce) slices Swiss cheese	½ teaspoon salt
4 (1-ounce) slices no-sugar-added ham	¼ teaspoon ground black pepper

1. Cut a 5"-long slit in the side of each chicken breast. Place a slice of Swiss and a slice of ham inside each slit. 2. Brush chicken with mustard, then sprinkle with salt and pepper on both sides. 3. Place chicken into the Crisper Tray. Slide the Crisper Tray into shelf position 4/5. Select the Chicken setting. Set the cooking temperature to 375°F and the cooking time to 25 minutes. Press Start/Pause to begin cooking, turning chicken halfway through cooking. 4. Chicken will be golden brown and have an internal temperature of at least 165°F when done. Serve warm.

Cheese Chicken Nuggets

Prep Time: 10 minutes | Cook Time: 15 minutes | Serves: 4

1-pound ground chicken thighs	½ teaspoon salt
½ cup shredded mozzarella cheese	¼ teaspoon dried oregano
1 large egg, whisked	¼ teaspoon garlic powder

1. In a large bowl, combine all ingredients. Form mixture into twenty nugget shapes, about 2 tablespoons each. 2. Place nuggets into the Crisper Tray, working in batches if needed. Slide the Crisper Tray into shelf position 4/5. Select the Air Fry setting. Set the cooking temperature to 375°F and the cooking time to 15 minutes. Press Start/Pause to begin cooking. Flip them halfway through the cooking time. 3. Let cool 5 minutes before serving.

Savory Garlic Ginger Chicken

Prep Time: 30 minutes | Cook Time: 12 minutes | Serves: 4

1 pound boneless, skinless chicken thighs, cut into 1" pieces	1 tablespoon minced ginger
¼ cup soy sauce	¼ teaspoon salt
2 cloves garlic, peeled and finely minced	

1. Place all ingredients in a large sealable bowl or bag. Place sealed bowl or bag into refrigerator and let marinate at least 30 minutes up to overnight. 2. Remove chicken from marinade and place into ungreased Crisper Tray. Slide the Crisper Tray into shelf position 4/5. Select the Chicken setting. Set the cooking temperature to 375°F and the cooking time to 12 minutes. Press Start/Pause to begin cooking, shaking the tray twice during cooking. 3. Chicken will be golden and have an internal temperature of at least 165°F when done. Serve warm.

Crispy Cajun Chicken Bites

Prep Time: 10 minutes | Cook Time: 12 minutes | Serves: 4

1 pound boneless, skinless chicken breasts, cut into 1" cubes	1 ounce plain pork rinds, finely crushed
½ cup heavy whipping cream	¼ cup unflavored whey protein powder
½ teaspoon salt	½ teaspoon Cajun seasoning
¼ teaspoon ground black pepper	

1. Place the chicken in a medium bowl and pour in the cream. Stir to coat. Sprinkle with salt and pepper. 2. In a separate large bowl, combine pork rinds, protein powder, and Cajun seasoning. Remove chicken from cream, shaking off any excess, and toss in dry mix until fully coated. 3. Place bites into ungreased Crisper Tray. Slide the Crisper Tray into shelf position 4/5. Select the Chicken setting. Set the cooking temperature to 400°F and the cooking time to 12 minutes. Press Start/Pause to begin cooking, shaking the tray twice during cooking. 4. Bites will be done when golden brown and have an internal temperature of at least 165°F. Serve warm.

Air Fryer Jerk Chicken Kebabs

Prep Time: 10 minutes | Cook Time: 14 minutes | Serves: 4

8 ounces chicken thighs, boneless, skinless, cut into 1" cubes
2 tablespoons jerk seasoning
2 tablespoons coconut oil

½ medium red bell pepper, seeded and cut into 1" pieces
¼ medium red onion, peeled and cut into 1" pieces
½ teaspoon salt

1. Place chicken in a medium bowl and sprinkle with jerk seasoning and coconut oil. Toss to coat on all sides. 2. Using eight 6" skewers, build skewers by alternating chicken, pepper, and onion pieces, about three repetitions per skewer. 3. Sprinkle salt over skewers and place into the Crisper Tray. Slide the Crisper Tray into shelf position 4/5. Select the Air Fry setting. Set the cooking temperature to 370°F and the cooking time to 14 minutes. Press Start/Pause to begin cooking. Flip them halfway through the cooking time. 4. Chicken will be golden and have an internal temperature of at least 165°F when done. Serve warm.

Gingered Turmeric Chicken Thighs

Prep Time: 5 minutes | Cook Time: 25 minutes | Serves: 4

4 (4-ounce) boneless, skin-on chicken thighs
2 tablespoons coconut oil, melted
½ teaspoon ground turmeric
½ teaspoon salt

½ teaspoon garlic powder
½ teaspoon ground ginger
¼ teaspoon ground black pepper

1. Add chicken thighs to a large bowl and drizzle with coconut oil. Sprinkle with remaining ingredients and stir to coat both sides of thighs. 2. Place thighs skin side up on the Crisper Tray and slide the Crisper Tray into shelf position 4/5. Select the Chicken setting. Set the cooking temperature to 400°F/204°C and the cooking time to 10 minutes. 3. After 10 minutes, turn thighs. When 5 minutes remain, flip thighs once more. 4. Chicken will be done when skin is golden brown and the internal temperature is at least 165°F. Serve warm.

Simple Mustard Chicken Wings

Prep Time: 5 minutes | Cook Time: 25 minutes | Serves: 4

1 pound bone-in chicken wings, separated at joints
¼ cup yellow mustard

½ teaspoon salt
¼ teaspoon ground black pepper

1. Place wings in a large bowl and toss with mustard to fully coat. Sprinkle with salt and pepper. 2. Place wings on the Crisper Tray and slide the Crisper Tray into shelf position 4/5. Select the Wings setting. Set the cooking temperature to 400°F/204°C and the cooking time to 25 minutes. Shake three times during cooking. 3. Wings will be done when browned and cooked to an internal temperature of at least 165°F. Serve warm.

Buffalo Chicken Meatballs

Prep Time: 5 minutes | Cook Time: 15 minutes | Serves: 4

1 pound ground chicken thighs
1 large egg, whisked
½ cup hot sauce, divided
½ cup crumbled blue cheese

2 tablespoons dry ranch seasoning
¼ teaspoon salt
¼ teaspoon ground black pepper

1. In a large bowl, combine egg, ground chicken, ¼ cup hot sauce, salt, blue cheese, ranch seasoning, and pepper. 2. Divide mixture into eight equal sections of about ¼ cup each and form each section into a ball. Place meatballs on the Crisper Tray and slide the Crisper Tray into shelf position 4/5. Select the Air Fry setting. Set the cooking temperature to 370°F/187°C and the cooking time to 15 minutes. 3. Meatballs will be done when golden and have an internal temperature of at least 165°F. 4. Transfer meatballs to a large serving dish and toss with remaining hot sauce. Serve warm.

Spicy Buffalo Chicken Tenders

Prep Time: 15 minutes | Cook Time: 20 minutes | Serves: 4

1 pound boneless, skinless chicken tenders
¼ cup hot sauce
1½ ounces pork rinds, finely ground

1 teaspoon chili powder
1 teaspoon garlic powder

1. Place chicken tenders in large bowl and pour hot sauce over them. Toss tenders in hot sauce, evenly coating. 2. In a separate large bowl, mix ground pork rinds with chili powder and garlic powder. 3. Place each tender in the ground pork rinds, covering completely. Wet your hands with water and press down the pork rinds into the chicken. 4. Place the tenders in a single layer on the Crisper Tray and slide the Crisper Tray into shelf position 4/5. 5. Select the Air Fry setting. Set the cooking temperature to 375°F/190°C and the cooking time to 20 minutes. 6. Serve warm.

Teriyaki Chicken Wings

Prep Time: 10 minutes | Cook Time: 25 minutes | Serves: 4

2 pounds chicken wings
½ cup sugar-free teriyaki sauce
2 teaspoons minced garlic

¼ teaspoon ground ginger
2 teaspoons baking powder

1. Place all ingredients except baking powder into a large bowl or bag and let marinade for 1 hour in the refrigerator. 2. Place wings on the Crisper Tray and sprinkle with baking powder. Gently rub into wings. Slide the Crisper Tray into shelf position 4/5. 3. Select the Wings setting. Set the cooking temperature to 400°F/204°C and the cooking time to 25 minutes. 4. Toss two or three times during cooking. 5. Wings should be crispy and cooked to at least 165°F internally when done. Serve immediately.

Flavorful Lemon Thyme Roasted Chicken

Prep Time: 10 minutes | Cook Time: 60 minutes | Serves: 6

1 (4-pound) chicken
2 teaspoons dried thyme
1 teaspoon garlic powder
½ teaspoon onion powder

2 teaspoons dried parsley
1 teaspoon baking powder
1 medium lemon
2 tablespoons salted butter, melted

1. Rub chicken with thyme, garlic powder, parsley, onion powder, and baking powder. 2. Slice lemon and place four slices on top of chicken, breast side up, and secure with toothpicks. Place remaining slices inside of the chicken. 3. Place entire chicken on the Baking Pan, breast side down, and slide the Baking Pan into shelf position 4/5. 4. Select the Chicken setting. Set the cooking temperature to 350°F/177°C and the cooking time to 60 minutes. 5. After 30 minutes, flip chicken so breast side is up. 6. When done, internal temperature should be 165°F and the skin golden and crispy. To serve, pour melted butter over entire chicken.

Limey Cilantro Chicken Thighs

Prep Time: 15 minutes | Cook Time: 22 minutes | Serves: 4

4 bone-in, skin-on chicken thighs
1 teaspoon baking powder
½ teaspoon garlic powder
2 teaspoons chili powder

1 teaspoon cumin
2 medium limes
¼ cup chopped fresh cilantro

1. Pat chicken thighs dry and sprinkle with baking powder. 2. In a small bowl, mix chili powder, garlic powder, and cumin and sprinkle evenly over thighs, gently rubbing on and under chicken skin. 3. Cut one lime in half and squeeze juice over thighs. Place chicken on the Baking Pan and slide the Baking Pan into shelf position 4/5. 4. Select the Chicken setting. Set the cooking temperature to 380°F/193°C and the cooking time to 22 minutes. 5. Cut other lime into four wedges for serving and garnish cooked chicken with wedges and cilantro.

Traditional Chicken Kiev

Prep Time: 15 minutes | Cook Time: 25 minutes | Serves: 4

1 cup (2 sticks) unsalted butter, softened (or butter-flavored coconut oil for dairy-free)	1 teaspoon fine sea salt, divided
	4 (4-ounce) boneless, skinless chicken breasts
2 tablespoons lemon juice	2 large eggs
2 tablespoons plus 1 teaspoon chopped fresh parsley leaves, divided, plus more for garnish	2 cups pork dust
	1 teaspoon ground black pepper
2 tablespoons chopped fresh tarragon leaves	Sprig of fresh parsley, for garnish
3 cloves garlic, minced	Lemon slices, for serving

1. Spray the Crisper Tray with avocado oil. 2. In a medium-sized bowl, combine the butter, lemon juice, 2 tablespoons of the parsley, tarragon, garlic, and ¼ teaspoon of the salt. Cover and place in the fridge to harden for 7 minutes. 3. While the butter mixture chills, place one of the chicken breasts on a cutting board. With a sharp knife held parallel to the cutting board, make a 1-inch-wide incision at the top of the breast. Carefully cut into the breast to form a large pocket, leaving a ½-inch border along the sides and bottom. Repeat with the other 3 breasts. 4. Stuff one-quarter of the butter mixture into each chicken breast and secure the openings with toothpicks. 5. Beat the eggs in a small shallow dish. In another shallow dish, combine the pork dust, the remaining 1 teaspoon of parsley, the remaining ¾ teaspoon of salt, and the pepper. 6. One at a time, dip the chicken breasts in the egg, shaking off the excess egg, and dredge the breasts in the pork dust mixture. Use your hands to press the pork dust onto each breast to form a nice crust. If you desire a thicker coating, dip it again in the egg and pork dust. As you finish, spray each coated chicken breast with avocado oil and place it on the Crisper Tray and slide the Tray into shelf position 4/5. 7. Select the Chicken setting. Set the cooking temperature to 350°F/176°C and the cooking time to 15 minutes. Flip the breasts and cook for an additional 10 minutes, or until the internal temperature of the chicken is 165°F and the crust is golden brown. 8. Serve garnished with the chopped fresh parsley and a parsley sprig, with lemon slices on the side. 9. Store leftovers in an airtight container in the refrigerator for up to 4 days or in the freezer for up to a month. Reheat in the Air Fryer at 350°F/176°C for 5 minutes, or until heated through.

Tasty Sesame Turkey Balls in Lettuce Cups

Prep Time: 10 minutes | Cook Time: 15 minutes | Serves: 6

Meatballs:

2 pounds ground turkey	amount of liquid or powdered sweetener
2 large eggs, beaten	2 teaspoons peeled and grated fresh ginger
¾ cup finely chopped button mushrooms	2 teaspoons toasted sesame oil
¼ cup finely chopped green onions, plus more for garnish if desired	1½ teaspoons wheat-free tamari, or 2 tablespoons coconut aminos
2 tablespoons Swerve confectioners'-style sweetener or equivalent	1 clove garlic, smashed to a paste

Sauce:

½ cup chicken broth	1 tablespoon lime juice
⅓ cup Swerve confectioners'-style sweetener or equivalent amount of liquid or powdered sweetener	¼ teaspoon peeled and grated fresh ginger
	1 clove garlic, smashed to a paste
2 tablespoons toasted sesame oil	Boston lettuce leaves, for serving
2 tablespoons tomato sauce	Sliced red chiles, for garnish (optional)
2 tablespoons wheat-free tamari, or ½ cup coconut aminos	Toasted sesame seeds, for garnish (optional)

1. Place all the ingredients for the meatballs in a large bowl and, using your hands, mix them together until well combined. Shape the mixture into about twelve 1½-inch meatballs and place them in a pie pan that fits in the appliance, leaving space between them. 2. Make the sauce: In a medium-sized bowl, mix together all the sauce ingredients until well combined. Pour the sauce over the meatballs. 3. Slide the Crisper Tray with the pan on top into shelf position 4/5. Select the Air Fry setting. Set the cooking temperature to 350°F/176°C and the cooking time to 15 minutes. Cook until the internal temperature of the meatballs reaches 165°F, flipping after 6 minutes. 4. To serve, lay several lettuce leaves on a serving plate and place several meatballs on top. Garnish with sliced red chiles, green onions, and/or sesame seeds, if desired. 5. Store leftovers in an airtight container in the refrigerator for up to 4 days or in the freezer for up to a month. Reheat in the Air Fryer at 350°F/176°C for 5 minutes, or until warmed through.

Classic Chicken Cordon Bleu Meatballs

Prep Time: 10 minutes | Cook Time: 15 minutes | Serves: 4

Meatballs:

½ pound ground chicken
½ pound ham, diced
½ cup finely grated Swiss cheese (about 2 ounces)
¼ cup chopped onions

3 cloves garlic, minced
1½ teaspoons fine sea salt
1 teaspoon ground black pepper, plus more for garnish if desired
1 large egg, beaten

Dijon Sauce:

¼ cup chicken broth, hot
3 tablespoons Dijon mustard
2 tablespoons lemon juice

¾ teaspoon fine sea salt
¼ teaspoon ground black pepper
Chopped fresh thyme leaves, for garnish (optional)

1. Spray the Crisper Tray with avocado oil. 2. In a large bowl, mix up all the ingredients for the meatballs with your hands until well combined. Shape the mixture into about twelve 1½-inch balls. Place the meatballs on the Crisper Tray, leaving space between them, and slide the Tray into shelf position 4/5. Select the Air Fry setting. Set the cooking temperature to 390°F/198°C and the cooking time to 15 minutes. Cook until cooked through and the internal temperature reaches 165°F. 3. While the meatballs cook, make the sauce: In a small mixing bowl, stir together all the sauce ingredients until well combined. 4. Pour the sauce into a serving dish. When the meatballs are cooked done, place them on top of sauce. Garnish with ground black pepper and fresh thyme leaves, if desired. 5. Store leftover meatballs in an airtight container in the refrigerator for up to 5 days or in the freezer for up to a month. Reheat in the Air Fryer at 350°F/176°C for 4 minutes, or until heated through.

Juicy Buffalo Chicken Drumsticks

Prep Time: 10 minutes | Cook Time: 25 minutes | Serves: 8

1 cup dill pickle juice
2 pounds chicken drumsticks

2 teaspoons fine sea salt

Wing Sauce:

⅓ cup hot sauce
¼ cup unsalted butter, melted
1 tablespoon lime juice

½ teaspoon fine sea salt
⅛ teaspoon garlic powder

For Serving:

½ cup Blue Cheese Dressing or Ranch Dressing

Celery sticks

1. Place the dill pickle juice in a large shallow dish and add the chicken. Spoon the juice over the chicken, cover, and place in the fridge to marinate for 2 hours or overnight. 2. Spray the Crisper Tray with avocado oil. 3. Pat the chicken dry and season well with the salt. Place the chicken on the Crisper Tray and slide the Tray into shelf position 4/5. Select the Chicken setting. Set the cooking temperature to 400°F/204°C and the cooking time to 20 minutes. Cook until the internal temperature reaches 165°F, flipping after 15 minutes. 4. While the chicken cooks, make the wing sauce: In a large mixing bowl, mix together all the sauce ingredients until well combined. 5. Remove the drumsticks and place them in the bowl with the sauce. Coat the drumsticks well with the sauce, then use tongs or a slotted spoon to place them on the Baking Pan, and cook in the Air Fryer for 5 minutes more. Serve with any extra wing sauce, blue cheese dressing, and celery sticks. 6. Store extra drumsticks in an airtight container in the fridge for up to 4 days or in the freezer for up to a month. Reheat in the Air Fryer at 350°F/176°C for 5 minutes, then increase the temperature to 400°F and cook for 3 to 5 minutes more, until warm and crispy.

Flavorful Porchetta–Style Chicken Breasts

Prep Time: 10 minutes | Cook Time: 15 minutes | Serves: 4

½ cup fresh parsley leaves
¼ cup roughly chopped fresh chives
4 cloves garlic, peeled
2 tablespoons lemon juice
3 teaspoons fine sea salt
1 teaspoon dried rubbed sage
1 teaspoon fresh rosemary leaves

1 teaspoon ground fennel
½ teaspoon red pepper flakes
4 (4-ounce) boneless, skinless chicken breasts, pounded to ¼ inch thick (see Tip)
8 slices bacon
Sprigs of fresh rosemary, for garnish (optional)

1. Spray the Baking Pan with avocado oil. 2. Place the parsley, chives, garlic, salt, sage, rosemary, lemon juice, fennel, and red pepper flakes in a food processor and puree until a smooth paste forms. 3. Place the chicken breasts on a cutting board and rub the paste all over the tops. With a short end facing you, roll each breast up like a jelly roll to make a log and secure it with toothpicks. 4. Wrap 2 slices of bacon around each chicken breast log to cover the entire breast. Secure the bacon with toothpicks. 5. Place the chicken breast logs in the Baking Pan and slide the Pan into shelf position 4/5. Select the Chicken setting. Set the cooking temperature to 340°F/171°C and the cooking time to 5 minutes. Then flip the logs over and cook for another 5 minutes. Increase the heat to 390°F/198°C and cook until the bacon is crisp, about 5 minutes more. 6. Remove the toothpicks and garnish with fresh rosemary sprigs, if desired, before serving. Store leftovers in an airtight container in the refrigerator for up to 4 days or in the freezer for up to a month. Reheat in the Air Fryer at 350°F/176°C for 5 minutes, then increase the heat to 390°F/198°C and cook for 2 minutes to crisp the bacon.

Thanksgiving Turkey Breast

Prep Time: 5 minutes | Cook Time: 30 minutes | Serves: 4

1½ teaspoons fine sea salt
1 teaspoon ground black pepper
1 teaspoon chopped fresh rosemary leaves
1 teaspoon chopped fresh sage
1 teaspoon chopped fresh tarragon

1 teaspoon chopped fresh thyme leaves
1 (2-pound) turkey breast
3 tablespoons ghee or unsalted butter, melted
3 tablespoons Dijon mustard

1. Spray the Baking Pan with avocado oil. 2. In a small bowl, mix together the salt, pepper, and herbs until well combined. Season the turkey breast generously on all sides with the seasoning. 3. In another small bowl, stir together the ghee and Dijon. Brush the ghee mixture on all sides of the turkey breast. 4. Place the turkey breast in the Baking Pan and slide the Pan into shelf position 4/5. Select the Chicken setting. Set the cooking temperature to 390°F/198°C and the cooking time to 30 minutes. Cook until the internal temperature reaches 165°F. Transfer the breast to a cutting board and allow it to rest for 10 minutes before cutting it into ½-inch-thick slices. 5. Store leftovers in an airtight container in the refrigerator for up to 4 days or in the freezer for up to a month. Reheat in the Air Fryer at 350°F/176°C for 4 minutes, or until warmed through.

Buttered Lemon Pepper Drumsticks

Prep Time: 5 minutes | Cook Time: 25 minutes | Serves: 4

2 teaspoons baking powder
½ teaspoon garlic powder
8 chicken drumsticks

4 tablespoons salted butter, melted
1 tablespoon lemon pepper seasoning

1. Sprinkle baking powder and garlic powder over drumsticks and rub into chicken skin. Place drumsticks on the Crisper Tray and slide the Crisper Tray into shelf position 4/5. 2. Select the Chicken setting. Set the cooking temperature to 375°F/190°C and the cooking time to 25 minutes. 3. Use tongs to turn drumsticks halfway through the cooking time. 4. When skin is golden and internal temperature is at least 165°F, remove from Crisper Tray. 5. In a large bowl, combine butter and lemon pepper seasoning. Add drumsticks to the bowl and toss until coated. Serve warm.

Chapter 5 Beef, Pork, and Lamb

Bacon Cheeseburger Casserole with Pickle Spears

Prep Time: 15 minutes | Cook Time: 20 minutes | Serves: 4

1 pound 80/20 ground beef	1 large egg
¼ medium white onion, peeled and chopped	4 slices sugar-free bacon, cooked and crumbled
1 cup shredded Cheddar cheese, divided	2 pickle spears, chopped

1. Brown the ground beef in a medium skillet over medium heat about 7–10 minutes. When no pink remains, drain the fat. Remove from heat and add ground beef to large mixing bowl. 2. Add onion, ½ cup Cheddar, and egg to bowl. Mix ingredients well and add crumbled bacon. 3. Pour the mixture into a 4-cup round baking dish that fits in the appliance and top with remaining Cheddar. Slide the Crisper Tray with the dish on top into shelf position 4/5. 4. Select the Air Fry setting. Set the cooking temperature to 375°F/190°C and the cooking time to 20 minutes. 5. Casserole will be golden on top and firm in the middle when fully cooked. Serve immediately with chopped pickles on top.

Pistachio–Crusted Rack of Lamb

Prep Time: 10 minutes | Cook Time: 19 minutes | Serves: 2

½ cup finely chopped pistachios	Salt and freshly ground black pepper
3 tablespoons panko breadcrumbs	1 tablespoon olive oil
1 teaspoon chopped fresh rosemary	1 rack of lamb, bones trimmed of fat and frenched
2 teaspoons chopped fresh oregano	1 tablespoon Dijon mustard

1. Combine the pistachios, breadcrumbs, oregano, salt, rosemary, and pepper in a small bowl. Drizzle in the olive oil and stir to combine. 2. Season the rack of lamb with pepper and salt on all sides and transfer it to the Crisper Tray with the fat side facing up. Slide the Crisper Tray into shelf position 4/5 with the Baking Pan placed underneath to catch drippings. 3. Select the Air Fry setting. Set the cooking temperature to 380°F/193°C and the cooking time to 12 minutes. 4. Remove the lamb and brush the fat side of the lamb rack with the Dijon mustard. Coat the rack with the pistachio mixture, pressing the breadcrumbs onto the lamb with your hands and rolling the bottom of the rack in any of the crumbs that fall off. 5. Return the rack of lamb to the Crisper Tray and cook for another 3 to 7 minutes or until an instant read thermometer reads 140°F for medium. Add or subtract a couple of minutes for lamb that is more or less well cooked. 6. Let the lamb rest for at least 5 minutes. Then, slice into chops and serve.

Lamb Koftas with Cucumber–Yogurt Dip

Prep Time: 10 minutes | Cook Time: 8 minutes | Serves: 3-4

1 pound ground lamb	1 egg, beaten
1 teaspoon ground cumin	½ teaspoon salt
1 teaspoon ground coriander	Freshly ground black pepper
2 tablespoons chopped fresh mint	
Cucumber-Yogurt Dip:	
½ English cucumber, grated (1 cup)	1 tablespoon olive oil
Salt	1 tablespoon chopped fresh dill
½ clove garlic, finely minced	Freshly ground black pepper
1 cup plain yogurt	

1. Add all ingredients to a bowl and mix together well. Divide the mixture into 10 portions. Roll each portion into a ball and then by cupping the meatball in your hand, shape it into an oval. 2. Place the koftas on the Crisper Tray and slide the Tray into shelf position 4/5. 3. Select the Air Fry setting. Set the cooking temperature to 400°F/204°C and the cooking time to 8 minutes. 4. When the koftas is cooking, make the cucumber-yogurt dip by placing the grated cucumber in a strainer and sprinkle with salt and letting this drain. Then combine the garlic, yogurt, oil and fresh dill in a bowl. Just before serving, stir the cucumber into the yogurt sauce and season to taste with freshly ground black pepper. 5. When the koftas is cooked done, serve warm with the cucumber-yogurt dip.

Crispy Marinated Pork Belly

Prep Time: 40 minutes | Cook Time: 20 minutes | Serves: 4

1 pound pork belly, cut into 1" cubes	2 teaspoons sriracha hot chili sauce
¼ cup soy sauce	½ teaspoon salt
1 tablespoon Worcestershire sauce	¼ teaspoon ground black pepper

1. Place pork belly into a medium sealable bowl or bag and pour in soy sauce, Worcestershire sauce, and sriracha. Seal and let marinate 30 minutes in the refrigerator. 2. Remove pork from marinade, pat dry with a paper towel, and sprinkle with pepper and salt. 3. Place pork on the Crisper Tray and slide the Tray into shelf position 4/5. 4. Select the Air Fry setting. Set the cooking temperature to 360°F/182°C and the cooking time to 20 minutes. Shake halfway through cooking. Pork belly will be done when it has an internal temperature of at least 145°F and is golden brown. 5. Let pork belly rest on a large plate 10 minutes. Serve warm.

Spicy Pulled Pork

Prep Time: 10 minutes | Cook Time: 2½ hours | Serves: 8

2 tablespoons chili powder	½ teaspoon ground black pepper
1 teaspoon garlic powder	½ teaspoon cumin
½ teaspoon onion powder	1 (4-pound) pork shoulder

1. In a small bowl, mix up chili powder, onion powder, garlic powder, pepper, and cumin. Rub the spice mixture over the pork shoulder, patting it into the skin. Place pork shoulder on the Crisper Tray and slide the Tray into shelf position 4/5. 2. Select the Air Fry setting. Set the cooking temperature to 350°F/176°C and the cooking time to 150 minutes. 3. Pork skin will be crispy and meat easily shredded with two forks when done. The internal temperature should be at least 145°F.

Barbecued Baby Back Ribs

Prep Time: 5 minutes | Cook Time: 25 minutes | Serves: 4

2 pounds baby back ribs	½ teaspoon garlic powder
2 teaspoons chili powder	¼ teaspoon ground cayenne pepper
1 teaspoon paprika	½ cup low-carb, sugar-free barbecue sauce
½ teaspoon onion powder	

1. Rub ribs with all ingredients except barbecue sauce. Place into Crisper Tray and slide the Tray into shelf position 6. 2. Select the Ribs setting. Set the cooking temperature to 400°F/204°C and the cooking time to 25 minutes. 3. When cooking is done, ribs will be dark and charred with an internal temperature of at least 190°F. Brush ribs with barbecue sauce and serve warm.

Tender Reverse Seared Ribeye

Prep Time: 5 minutes | Cook Time: 45 minutes | Serves: 2

1 (8-ounce) ribeye steak	1 tablespoon salted butter, softened
½ teaspoon pink Himalayan salt	¼ teaspoon garlic powder
¼ teaspoon ground peppercorn	½ teaspoon dried parsley
1 tablespoon coconut oil	¼ teaspoon dried oregano

1. Rub steak with salt and ground peppercorn. Place the steak on the Wire Rack and slide the Wire Rack into shelf position 2 with the Baking Pan placed underneath to catch drippings. 2. Select the Steak setting. Set the cooking temperature to 250°F/121°C and the cooking time to 45 minutes. 3. When the cooking is complete, begin checking doneness and add a few minutes until internal temperature is your personal preference. 4. In a medium skillet over medium heat, heat coconut oil. When oil is hot, quickly sear outside and sides of steak until crisp and browned. Remove from heat and let steak rest. 5. In a small bowl, whip butter with garlic powder, parsley, and oregano. 6. Slice steak and serve with herb butter on top.

Mouthwatering Pub–Style Burger

Prep Time: 10 minutes | Cook Time: 10 minutes | Serves: 4

1 pound ground sirloin	2 teaspoons sriracha
½ teaspoon salt	¼ teaspoon garlic powder
¼ teaspoon ground black pepper	8 large leaves butter lettuce
2 tablespoons salted butter, melted	4 Bacon-Wrapped Onion Rings
½ cup full-fat mayonnaise	8 slices pickle

1. In a medium bowl, combine salt, ground sirloin, and pepper. Form four patties. Brush each with butter and then place on the Crisper Tray and slide the Tray into shelf position 4/5. 2. Select the Air Fry setting. Set the cooking temperature to 380°F/193°C and the cooking time to 10 minutes. 3. Flip the patties halfway through the cooking time for a medium burger. Add an additional 3–5 minutes for well-done. 4. In a small bowl, mix up mayonnaise, sriracha, and garlic powder. Set aside. 5. Place each cooked burger on a lettuce leaf and top with onion ring, two pickles, and dollop of your prepared burger sauce. Wrap another lettuce leaf around tightly to hold. Serve warm.

Crispy Reuben Fritters

Prep Time: 10 minutes | Cook Time: 16 minutes | Serves: 6

2 cups finely diced cooked corned beef	Chopped fresh thyme, for garnish
1 (8-ounce) package cream cheese, softened	Thousand Island Dipping Sauce, for serving (optional; omit for egg-free)
½ cup finely shredded Swiss cheese (about 2 ounces)	
¼ cup sauerkraut	Cornichons, for serving (optional)
1 cup pork dust or powdered Parmesan cheese	

1. Spray the Crisper Tray with avocado oil. 2. In a large bowl, mix together the corned beef, Swiss cheese, cream cheese, and sauerkraut until well combined. Form the corned beef mixture into twelve 1½-inch balls. 3. Place the pork dust in a shallow bowl. Roll the corned beef balls in the pork dust and use your hands to form it into a thick crust around each ball. 4. Place 6 balls on the Crisper Tray, spaced about ½ inch apart, and slide the Crisper Tray into shelf position 4/5. Select the Air Fry setting. Set the cooking temperature to 390°F/198°C and the cooking time to 8 minutes. Cook until golden brown and crispy. Allow them to cool a bit before lifting them out of the air fryer (the fritters are very soft when the cheese is melted; they're easier to handle once the cheese has hardened a bit). Repeat with the remaining fritters. 5. Garnish with chopped fresh thyme and serve with the dipping sauce and cornichons, if desired. Store leftovers in an airtight container in the fridge for 3 days or in the freezer for up to a month. Reheat in the air fryer at 350°F/176°C for 4 minutes, or until heated through.

Greek Stuffed Beef Tenderloin

Prep Time: 10 minutes | Cook Time: 10 minutes | Serves: 4

1½ pounds venison or beef tenderloin, pounded to ¼ inch thick	½ cup crumbled feta cheese (about 2 ounces)
3 teaspoons fine sea salt	¼ cup finely chopped onions
1 teaspoon ground black pepper	2 cloves garlic, minced
2 ounces creamy goat cheese	
For Garnish/Serving (Optional):	
Prepared yellow mustard	Sprigs of fresh rosemary
Halved cherry tomatoes	Lavender flowers
Extra-virgin olive oil	

1. Spray the Baking Pan with avocado oil. 2. Season tenderloin on all sides with pepper and salt. 3. In a medium-sized mixing bowl, combine the onions, feta, goat cheese, and garlic. Place the mixture in the center of the tenderloin. Starting at the end closest to you, tightly roll the tenderloin like a jelly roll. Tie the rolled tenderloin tightly with kitchen twine. 4. Place the meat on the Baking Pan and slide the Baking Pan into shelf position 4/5. Select the Air Fry setting. Set the cooking temperature to 400°F/204°C and the cooking time to 5 minutes. Flip the meat over and cook for an additional 5 minutes, or until the internal temperature reaches 135°F for medium-rare. 5. To serve, smear a line of prepared yellow mustard on a platter, then place the meat next to it and add halved cherry tomatoes on the side, if desired. Drizzle with the olive oil and garnish with the rosemary sprigs and lavender flowers, if desired. 6. Best served fresh. Store leftovers in an airtight container in the fridge for 3 days. Reheat in the air fryer at 350°F/176°C for 4 minutes, or until heated through.

Delicious Herb–Crusted Lamb Chops

Prep Time: 10 minutes | Cook Time: 5 minutes | Serves: 2

1 large egg
2 cloves garlic, minced
¼ cup pork dust
¼ cup powdered Parmesan cheese (or pork dust for dairy-free)
1 tablespoon chopped fresh oregano leaves
For Garnish/Serving (Optional):
Sprigs of fresh oregano
Sprigs of fresh rosemary
Sprigs of fresh thyme

1 tablespoon chopped fresh rosemary leaves
1 teaspoon chopped fresh thyme leaves
½ teaspoon ground black pepper
4 (1-inch-thick) lamb chops

Lavender flowers
Lemon slices

1. Spray the Crisper Tray with avocado oil. 2. Beat the egg in a shallow bowl and stir in the garlic until combine well. In another shallow bowl, mix together the pork dust, Parmesan, herbs, and pepper. 3. One at a time, dip the lamb chops into the egg mixture, shake off the excess egg, and then dredge them in the Parmesan mixture. Use your hands to coat the chops well in the Parmesan mixture and form a nice crust on all sides; if necessary, dip the chops again in both the egg and the Parmesan mixture. 4. Place the lamb chops on the Crisper Tray, leaving space between them, and slide the Crisper Tray into shelf position 4/5. Select the Air Fry setting. Set the cooking temperature to 400°F/204°C and the cooking time to 5 minutes. Cook until the internal temperature reaches 145°F for medium doneness. Let rest for 10 minutes before serving. 5. Garnish with sprigs of oregano, rosemary, and thyme, and lavender flowers, if desired. Serve with lemon slices, if desired. 6. Best served fresh. Store leftovers in an airtight container in the fridge for up to 4 days. Serve chilled over a salad, or reheat in the air fryer at 350°F/176°C for 3 minutes, or until heated through.

Best Black 'n' Blue Burgers

Prep Time: 5 minutes | Cook Time: 10 minutes | Serves: 2

½ teaspoon fine sea salt
¼ teaspoon ground black pepper
¼ teaspoon garlic powder
¼ teaspoon onion powder
¼ teaspoon smoked paprika
2 (¼-pound) hamburger patties, ½ inch thick

½ cup crumbled blue cheese (about 2 ounces) (omit for dairy-free)
2 Hamburger Buns
2 tablespoons mayonnaise
6 red onion slices
2 Boston lettuce leaves

1. Spray the Crisper Tray with avocado oil. 2. In a small bowl, combine the pepper, salt, and seasonings. Season the patties well on both sides with the seasoning mixture. 3. Place the patties on the Crisper Tray and slide the Crisper Tray into shelf position 4/5. Select the Air Fry setting. Set the cooking temperature to 360°F/182°C and the cooking time to 7 minutes. Cook until the internal temperature reaches 145°F for a medium-done burger. Place the blue cheese on top of the patties and cook for another minute to melt the cheese. Remove the burgers and allow to rest for 5 minutes. 4. Slice the buns in half and smear 2 halves with a tablespoon of mayo each. Place the buns on the Wire Rack cut side up and slide the Wire Rack into shelf position 4/5. Select the Toast setting and toast the buns at 400°F/204°C for 1 to 2 minutes, until golden brown. 5. Remove the buns and place them on a serving plate. Place the burgers on the buns and top each burger with 3 red onion slices and a lettuce leaf. 6. Best served fresh. Store leftover patties in an airtight container in the fridge for 3 days or in the freezer for up to a month. Reheat in the air fryer at 350°F/176°C for 4 minutes, or until heated through.

Juicy Blackened Steak Nuggets

Prep Time: 10 minutes | Cook Time: 7 minutes | Serves: 2

1 pound rib eye steak, cut into 1" cubes
2 tablespoons salted butter, melted
½ teaspoon paprika
½ teaspoon salt

¼ teaspoon garlic powder
¼ teaspoon onion powder
¼ teaspoon ground black pepper
⅛ teaspoon cayenne pepper

1. Place steak into a large bowl and pour in butter. Toss to coat. Sprinkle with remaining ingredients. 2. Place bites on the Baking Pan and slide the Baking Pan into shelf position 4/5. Select the Air Fry setting. Set the cooking temperature to 400°F/204°C and the cooking time to 7 minutes. Shake three times during cooking. 3. Steak will be crispy on the outside and browned when done and internal temperature is at least 150°F for medium and 180°F for well-done. Serve warm.

Sweet–Spicy Pork Spare Ribs

Prep Time: 10 minutes | Cook Time: 30 minutes | Serves: 6

¼ cup granular brown erythritol
2 teaspoons paprika
2 teaspoons chili powder
1 teaspoon garlic powder

½ teaspoon cayenne pepper
2 teaspoons salt
1 teaspoon ground black pepper
1 (4-pound) rack pork spare ribs

1. In a small bowl, mix erythritol, paprika, chili powder, cayenne pepper, salt, garlic powder, and black pepper. Rub spice mix over ribs on both sides. Place ribs on ungreased aluminum foil sheet and wrap to cover. 2. Place ribs on the Crisper Tray and slide the Crisper Tray into shelf position 6. Select the Ribs setting. Set the cooking temperature to 400°F/204°C and the cooking time to 25 minutes. 3. When the cooking is complete, remove ribs from foil, then place back into air fryer to cook an additional 5 minutes, turning halfway through cooking. 4. Ribs will be browned and have an internal temperature of at least 180°F when done. Serve warm.

Homemade Mojito Lamb Chops

Prep Time: 5 minutes | Cook Time: 5 minutes | Serves: 2

4 (1-inch-thick) lamb chops
Sprigs of fresh mint, for garnish (optional)
Marinade:
2 teaspoons grated lime zest
½ cup lime juice
¼ cup avocado oil
¼ cup chopped fresh mint leaves

Lime slices, for serving (optional)

4 cloves garlic, roughly chopped
2 teaspoons fine sea salt
½ teaspoon ground black pepper

1. Make the marinade by placing all the ingredients for marinade in a food processor or blender and puree until mostly smooth with a few small chunks. Transfer half of the marinade to a shallow dish and set the other half aside for serving. Add the lamb to the shallow dish, cover, and put in the refrigerator to marinate for at least 2 hours or overnight. 2. Spray the Crisper Tray with avocado oil. 3. Remove the chops from the marinade, place them on the Crisper Tray, and slide the Crisper Tray into shelf position 4/5. Select the Air Fry setting. Set the cooking temperature to 390°F/198°C and the cooking time to 5 minutes. Cook until the internal temperature reaches 145°F for medium doneness. 4. Allow the chops to rest for 10 minutes before serving with the rest of the marinade as a sauce. Garnish with the fresh mint leaves and serve with the lime slices, if desired. Best served fresh.

Tasty Mushroom Swiss Burgers

Prep Time: 5 minutes | Cook Time: 15 minutes | Serves: 2

2 large portobello mushrooms
1 teaspoon fine sea salt, divided
¼ teaspoon garlic powder
¼ teaspoon ground black pepper
¼ teaspoon onion powder

¼ teaspoon smoked paprika
2 (¼-pound) hamburger patties, ½ inch thick
2 slices Swiss cheese (omit for dairy-free)
Condiments of choice, such as Ranch Dressing (use dairy-free if needed), prepared yellow mustard, or mayonnaise, for serving

1. Clean the portobello mushrooms and remove the stems. Spray the mushrooms on all sides with avocado oil and season them with ½ teaspoon of the salt. 2. Place the mushrooms on the Crisper Tray and slide the Crisper Tray into shelf position 4/5. Select the Vegetables setting. Set the cooking temperature to 360°F/182°C and the cooking time to 8 minutes. Cook for 7 to 8 minutes, until fork-tender and soft to the touch. 3. While the mushrooms cook, in a small bowl mix together the remaining ½ teaspoon of salt, the garlic powder, pepper, onion powder, and paprika. Sprinkle the hamburger patties with the seasoning mixture. 4. When the mushrooms are done cooking, remove them and place them on a serving platter with the cap side down. 5. Place the hamburger patties on the Crisper Tray and slide the Crisper Tray into shelf position 4/5. Select the Air Fry setting. Set the cooking temperature to 360°F/182°C and the cooking time to 7 minutes. Cook until the internal temperature reaches 145°F for a medium-done burger. Place a slice of Swiss cheese on each patty and cook for another minute to melt the cheese. 6. Place the burgers on top of the mushrooms and drizzle with condiments of your choice. Best served fresh.

Mouthwatering Keto Turtles

Prep Time: 15 minutes | Cook Time: 15 minutes | Serves: 4

1 pound ground beef	8 whole peppercorns
1 teaspoon fine sea salt	2 large dill pickles
½ teaspoon ground black pepper	2 slices bacon
4 hot dogs	
For Serving:	
Prepared yellow mustard	Cornichons

1. Spray the Crisper Tray with avocado oil. 2. Create the turtle shells: Form the ground beef into 4 equal-sized patties. Season the outsides of patties with the pepper and salt. 3. Make the turtle heads: Slice 1½ inches off one end of each hot dog. Use your thumb to make an indent in the side of each ground beef patty and press in a hot dog end for the head. Score 2 spots in each hot dog end for the eyes with the tip of a sharp knife. Place a whole peppercorn in each slot. 4. Make the turtle legs: Cut the rest of the hot dogs in half lengthwise, then cut each half in half crosswise (you should have sixteen 1½-inch pieces). Place one piece flat side down under each front corner of the patties. You will have 8 hot dog pieces left over. 5. Decorate the shells: Cut the dill pickles into ⅛-inch-thick slices that are about 3 inches long. Place the pickle slices parallel to each other on top of the ground beef patties, spaced about half an inch apart. 6. Slice the bacon into ¼-inch-wide and 5- to 6-inch-long strips. Place the strips on the patties, on top of and perpendicular to the pickle slices, spaced about half an inch apart. Tuck the ends of the bacon strips underneath the turtle so they don't curl up. 7. Working in batches if necessary, place the turtles on the Crisper Tray, leaving space between them, and slide the Crisper Tray into shelf position 4/5 with the Baking Pan placed underneath to catch drippings. Select the Air Fry setting. Set the cooking temperature to 390°F/198°C and the cooking time to 15 minutes. Cook until the beef is cooked to your liking. 8. Remove from the air fryer and serve with mustard and cornichons. Store leftovers in an airtight container in the refrigerator for up to 4 days or in the freezer for up to 2 months. Reheat in the air fryer at 390°F/198°C for about 5 minutes, until heated through.

Barbecued Pork Spare Ribs

Prep Time: 10 minutes | Cook Time: 30 minutes | Serves: 4

1 (4-pound) rack pork spare ribs	1 teaspoon garlic powder
1 teaspoon ground cumin	½ teaspoon dry ground mustard
2 teaspoons salt	½ cup low-carb barbecue sauce
1 teaspoon ground black pepper	

1. Place ribs on ungreased aluminum foil sheet. Carefully use a knife to remove membrane and sprinkle meat evenly on both sides with cumin, salt, garlic powder, pepper, and ground mustard. 2. Cut rack into portions that will fit in the appliance, and wrap each portion in one layer of aluminum foil, working in batches if needed. 3. Place ribs on the Crisper Tray and slide the Crisper Tray into shelf position 6. Select the Ribs setting. Set the cooking temperature to 400°F/204°C and the cooking time to 25 minutes. 4. When the cooking is complete, carefully remove ribs from foil and brush them with barbecue sauce. Return to air fryer and cook at 400°F/204°C for an additional 5 minutes to brown. Ribs will be done when no pink remains and internal temperature is at least 180°F. Serve warm.

Parmesan Italian Meatballs

Prep Time: 10 minutes | Cook Time: 20 minutes | Serves: 4

1 pound 80/20 ground beef	½ teaspoon dried parsley
1 large egg, whisked	¼ teaspoon ground black pepper
¼ cup grated Parmesan cheese	¼ teaspoon dried oregano
½ teaspoon salt	

1. In a large bowl, mix up all ingredients. Scoop out 3 tablespoons mixture and roll into a ball. Repeat with remaining mixture to form sixteen balls total. 2. Place meatballs on the Crisper Tray in a single layer, working in batches if needed, and slide the Crisper Tray into shelf position 4/5. Select the Air Fry setting. Set the cooking temperature to 400°F/204°C and the cooking time to 20 minutes. Shake halfway through cooking. 3. Meatballs will be browned and have an internal temperature of at least 180°F when done. Serve warm.

Rosemary Roast Beef

Prep Time: 5 minutes | Cook Time: 60 minutes | Serves: 6

1 (2-pound) top round beef roast	1 teaspoon dried rosemary
1 teaspoon salt	½ teaspoon garlic powder
½ teaspoon ground black pepper	1 tablespoon coconut oil, melted

1. Sprinkle all sides of roast with salt, rosemary, pepper, and garlic powder. Drizzle with coconut oil. Place roast on the Baking Pan, fatty side down, and slide the Baking Pan into shelf position 4/5. 2. Select the Air Fry setting. Set the cooking temperature to 375°F/190°C and the cooking time to 60 minutes. 3. Turn the roast halfway through cooking. 4. Roast will be done when no pink remains and internal temperature is at least 180°F. Serve warm.

Mexican Shredded Beef

Prep Time: 5 minutes | Cook Time: 35 minutes | Serves: 6

1 (2-pound) beef chuck roast, cut into 2" cubes	½ teaspoon ground black pepper
1 teaspoon salt	½ cup no-sugar-added chipotle sauce

1. In a large bowl, sprinkle beef cubes with pepper and salt and toss to coat. Place beef on the Crisper Tray and slide the Crisper Tray into shelf position 4/5. 2. Select the Air Fry setting. Set the cooking temperature to 400°F/204°C and the cooking time to 30 minutes. Shake halfway through cooking. 3. Beef will be done when internal temperature is at least 160°F. 4. Place cooked beef into a large bowl and shred with two forks. Pour in chipotle sauce and toss to coat. 5. Return beef to the Crisper Tray and cook for another 5 minutes at 400°F/204°C to crisp with sauce. Serve warm.

Scallion Pork Meatballs

Prep Time: 20 minutes | Cook Time: 12 minutes | Serves: 6

1 pound ground pork	½ teaspoon ground ginger
1 large egg, whisked	¼ teaspoon crushed red pepper flakes
½ teaspoon garlic powder	1 medium scallion, trimmed and sliced
½ teaspoon salt	

1. Mix up all ingredients in a large bowl. Spoon out 2 tablespoons mixture and roll into a ball. Repeat to form eighteen meatballs total. 2. Place meatballs on the Crisper Tray and slide the Crisper Tray into shelf position 4/5. Select the Air Fry setting. Set the cooking temperature to 400°F/204°C and the cooking time to 12 minutes. Shake three times throughout cooking. 3. Meatballs will be browned and have an internal temperature of at least 145°F when done. Serve warm.

Garlic London Broil

Prep Time: 10 minutes | Cook Time: 12 minutes | Serves: 4

1 pound top round steak	½ teaspoon ground black pepper
1 tablespoon Worcestershire sauce	½ teaspoon salt
¼ cup soy sauce	2 tablespoons salted butter, melted
2 cloves garlic, peeled and finely minced	

1. Place steak in a large sealable bowl or bag. Pour in Worcestershire sauce and soy sauce, then add pepper, garlic, and salt. Toss to coat. Seal and place into refrigerator to let marinate for 2 hours. 2. Remove the steak from marinade and pat dry. Drizzle top side with butter, then place on the Crisper Tray and slide the Crisper Tray into shelf position 4/5. Select the Air Fry setting. Set the cooking temperature to 375°F/190°C and the cooking time to 12 minutes. Turn steak halfway through cooking. 3. Steak will be done when browned at the edges and it has an internal temperature of 150°F for medium or 180°F for well-done. 4. Let steak rest on a large plate 10 minutes before slicing into thin pieces. Serve warm.

Savory Spice–Rubbed Pork Loin

Prep Time: 5 minutes | Cook Time: 20 minutes | Serves: 6

1 teaspoon paprika	2 tablespoons coconut oil
½ teaspoon ground cumin	1 (1½-pound) boneless pork loin
½ teaspoon chili powder	½ teaspoon salt
½ teaspoon garlic powder	¼ teaspoon ground black pepper

1. In a small bowl, mix chili powder, paprika, cumin, and garlic powder. 2. Drizzle coconut oil over pork. Sprinkle pork loin with salt and pepper, then rub spice mixture evenly on all sides. 3. Place pork on the Crisper Tray and slide the Crisper Tray into shelf position 4/5. Select the Air Fry setting. Set the cooking temperature to 400°F/204°C and the cooking time to 20 minutes. Turn pork halfway through cooking. 4. Pork loin will be browned and have an internal temperature of at least 145°F when done. Serve warm.

Hearty Bacon and Blue Cheese Burgers

Prep Time: 10 minutes | Cook Time: 15 minutes | Serves: 4

1 pound 70/30 ground beef	¼ cup peeled and chopped yellow onion
6 slices cooked sugar-free bacon, finely chopped	½ teaspoon salt
½ cup crumbled blue cheese	¼ teaspoon ground black pepper

1. In a large bowl, mix ground beef, blue cheese, bacon, and onion. Separate into four sections and shape each section into a patty. Sprinkle with salt and pepper. 2. Place patties on the Crisper Tray and slide the Crisper Tray into shelf position 4/5. Select the Air Fry setting. Set the cooking temperature to 350°F/176°C and the cooking time to 15 minutes. Turn patties halfway through cooking. 3. Burgers will be done when internal temperature is at least 150°F for medium and 180°F for well. Serve warm.

Tender Swedish Meatloaf

Prep Time: 10 minutes | Cook Time: 35 minutes | Serves: 8

1½ pounds ground beef (85% lean)	2 tablespoons dry mustard
¼ pound ground pork	2 cloves garlic, minced
1 large egg (omit for egg-free)	2 teaspoons fine sea salt
½ cup minced onions	1 teaspoon ground black pepper, plus more for garnish
¼ cup tomato sauce	
Sauce:	
½ cup (1 stick) unsalted butter	⅓ cup beef broth
½ cup shredded Swiss or mild cheddar cheese (about 2 ounces)	⅛ teaspoon ground nutmeg
2 ounces cream cheese (¼ cup), softened	Halved cherry tomatoes, for serving (optional)

1. In a large bowl, combine the ground beef, egg, onions, dry mustard, garlic, tomato sauce, salt, ground pork, and pepper. Using your hands, mix until well combined. 2. Place the meatloaf mixture in a 9 by 5-inch loaf pan that fits in the appliance. 3. Slide the Crisper Tray with the pan on top into shelf position 4/5. Select the Air Fry setting. Set the cooking temperature to 390°F/198°C and the cooking time to 35 minutes. Cook until cooked through and the internal temperature reaches 145°F. Check the meatloaf after 25 minutes; if it's getting too brown on the top, cover it loosely with foil to prevent burning. 4. While the meatloaf cooks, make the sauce: Heat the butter in a saucepan over medium-high heat until it sizzles and brown flecks appear, stirring constantly to keep it from burning. Turn the heat down to low and whisk in the Swiss cheese, broth, cream cheese, and nutmeg. Simmer for at least 10 minutes. The longer it simmers, the more the flavors open up. 5. When the meatloaf is done, transfer it to a serving tray and pour the sauce over it. Garnish with ground black pepper and serve with cherry tomatoes, if desired. Allow the meatloaf to rest for 10 minutes before slicing so it doesn't crumble apart. 6. Store leftovers in an airtight container in the fridge for 3 days or in the freezer for up to a month. Reheat in the Air Fryer at 350°F/176°C for 4 minutes, or until heated through.

Fresh Spinach and Provolone Steak Rolls

Prep Time: 10 minutes | Cook Time: 12 minutes | Serves: 4

1 (1-pound) flank steak, butterflied
8 (1-ounce, ¼"-thick) deli slices provolone cheese
1 cup fresh spinach leaves

½ teaspoon salt
¼ teaspoon ground black pepper

1. Place steak on a large plate. Place provolone slices to cover steak, leaving 1" at the edges. Lay spinach leaves over cheese. Gently roll steak and tie with kitchen twine or secure with toothpicks. Carefully slice into eight pieces. Sprinkle each with salt and pepper. 2. Place rolls on the Baking Pan, cut side up, and slide the Baking Pan into shelf position 4/5. Select the Air Fry setting. Set the cooking temperature to 400°F/204°C and the cooking time to 12 minutes. 3. Steak rolls will be browned and cheese will be melted when done and have an internal temperature of at least 150°F for medium steak and 180°F for well-done steak. Serve warm.

Traditional Mini Meatloaf

Prep Time: 10 minutes | Cook Time: 25 minutes | Serves: 6

1 pound 80/20 ground beef
¼ medium yellow onion, peeled and diced
½ medium green bell pepper, seeded and diced
1 large egg
3 tablespoons blanched finely ground almond flour
1 tablespoon Worcestershire sauce

½ teaspoon garlic powder
1 teaspoon dried parsley
2 tablespoons tomato paste
¼ cup water
1 tablespoon powdered erythritol

1. In a large bowl, combine pepper, ground beef, onion, egg, and almond flour. Pour in the Worcestershire sauce and add the garlic powder and parsley to the bowl. Mix until fully combined. 2. Divide the mixture into two and place into two (4") loaf baking pans that fit in the appliance. 3. In a small bowl, combine the tomato paste, water, and erythritol. Spoon half the mixture over each loaf. 4. Working in batches, slide the Crisper Tray with the dish on top into shelf position 4/5. 5. Select the Air Fry setting. Set the cooking temperature to 350°F/176°C and the cooking time to 25 minutes. Cook until internal temperature is 180°F. 6. Serve warm.

Spicy Chorizo and Beef Burger

Prep Time: 10 minutes | Cook Time: 15 minutes | Serves: 4

¾ pound 80/20 ground beef
¼ pound Mexican-style ground chorizo
¼ cup chopped onion
5 slices pickled jalapeños, chopped

2 teaspoons chili powder
1 teaspoon minced garlic
¼ teaspoon cumin

1. In a large bowl, mix up all ingredients. Divide the mixture into four sections and form them into burger patties. 2. Working in batches if necessary, place burger patties on the Crisper Tray and slide the Crisper Tray into shelf position 4/5. 3. Select the Air Fry setting. Set the cooking temperature to 375°F/190°C and the cooking time to 15 minutes. 4. Flip the patties halfway through the cooking time. Serve warm.

Easy Crispy Brats

Prep Time: 5 minutes | Cook Time: 15 minutes | Serves: 4

4 (3-ounce) beef bratwursts

1. Place brats on the Crisper Tray and slide the Crisper Tray into shelf position 4/5. 2. Select the Air Fry setting. Set the cooking temperature to 375°F/190°C and the cooking time to 15 minutes. 3. Serve warm.

Cumin Taco–Stuffed Peppers

Prep Time: 15 minutes | Cook Time: 15 minutes | Serves: 4

1 pound 80/20 ground beef
1 tablespoon chili powder
2 teaspoons cumin
1 teaspoon garlic powder
1 teaspoon salt

¼ teaspoon ground black pepper
1 (10-ounce) can diced tomatoes and green chiles, drained
4 medium green bell peppers
1 cup shredded Monterey jack cheese, divided

1. In a medium skillet, brown the ground beef over medium heat for about 7 to 10 minutes. When no pink remains, drain the fat from the skillet. 2. Return the skillet to the stovetop and add chili powder, cumin, salt, garlic powder, and black pepper. Add drained can of diced tomatoes and chiles to the skillet. Continue cooking for 3 to 5 minutes. 3. While the mixture is cooking, cut each bell pepper in half. Remove the seeds and white membrane. Spoon the cooked mixture evenly into each bell pepper and top with a ¼ cup cheese. Place stuffed peppers on the Crisper Tray and slide the Crisper Tray into shelf position 4/5. 4. Select the Air Fry setting. Set the cooking temperature to 350°F/176°C and the cooking time to 15 minutes. 5. When done, peppers will be fork tender and cheese will be browned and bubbling. Serve warm.

Italian Sausage Stuffed Bell Peppers

Prep Time: 15 minutes | Cook Time: 15 minutes | Serves: 4

1 pound ground pork Italian sausage
½ teaspoon garlic powder
½ teaspoon dried parsley
1 medium Roma tomato, diced

¼ cup chopped onion
4 medium green bell peppers
1 cup shredded mozzarella cheese, divided

1. In a medium skillet, brown the ground sausage over medium heat for about 7 to 10 minutes or until no pink remains. Drain the fat from the skillet. 2. Return the skillet to the stovetop and add garlic powder, tomato, parsley, and onion. Continue cooking for 3 to 5 minutes. 3. Slice peppers in half and remove the seeds and white membrane. 4. Remove the meat mixture from the stovetop and spoon evenly into pepper halves. Top with mozzarella. Place pepper halves on the Crisper Tray and slide the Crisper Tray into shelf position 4/5. 5 Select the Air Fry setting. Set the cooking temperature to 350°F/176°C and the cooking time to 15 minutes. 6. When done, peppers will be fork tender and cheese will be golden. Serve warm.

Tasty Salisbury Steak with Mushroom Onion Gravy

Prep Time: 10 minutes | Cook Time: 33 minutes | Serves: 2

Mushroom Onion Gravy:
¾ cup sliced button mushrooms
¼ cup thinly sliced onions
¼ cup unsalted butter, melted (or bacon fat for dairy-free)
Steaks:
½ pound ground beef (85% lean)
¼ cup minced onions, or ½ teaspoon onion powder
2 tablespoons tomato paste
1 tablespoon dry mustard

½ teaspoon fine sea salt
¼ cup beef broth

1 clove garlic, minced, or ¼ teaspoon garlic powder
½ teaspoon fine sea salt
¼ teaspoon ground black pepper, plus more for garnish if desired
Chopped fresh thyme leaves, for garnish (optional)

1. Make the gravy by placing the mushrooms and onions in a casserole dish that fits in the appliance. Pour the melted butter on top of them and stir to coat, then season with the salt. Place the dish Slide the Crisper Tray with the dish on top into shelf position 4/5. 2. Select the Air Fry setting. Set the cooking temperature to 390°F/198°C and the cooking time to 5 minutes. Stir and cook for another 3 minutes, or until the onions are soft and the mushrooms are browning. Add the broth and cook for an additional 10 minutes. 3. While the gravy is cooking, prepare the steaks by adding the ground beef, onions, tomato paste, dry mustard, garlic, salt, and pepper in a large bowl and mix together until well combined. Form the mixture into 2 oval-shaped patties. 4. Place the patties on top of the mushroom gravy. Cook for 10 minutes, gently flip the patties, then cook for another 2 to 5 minutes, until the beef is cooked through and the internal temperature reaches 145°F. 5. Transfer the steaks to a serving platter and pour the gravy over them. Garnish with the ground black pepper and chopped fresh thyme, if desired. Store leftovers in an airtight container in the fridge for 3 days or in the freezer for up to a month. Reheat in the Air Fryer at 350°F/176°C for 4 minutes, or until heated through.

Delicious Beefy Poppers

Prep Time: 15 minutes | Cook Time: 15 minutes | Serves: 4

8 medium jalapeño peppers, stemmed, halved, and seeded	1 teaspoon fine sea salt
1 (8-ounce) package cream cheese (or Kite Hill brand cream cheese style spread for dairy-free), softened	½ teaspoon ground black pepper
	8 slices thin-cut bacon
2 pounds ground beef (85% lean)	Fresh cilantro leaves, for garnish

1. Spray the Baking Pan with avocado oil. 2. Stuff each jalapeño half with a few tablespoons of cream cheese. Place the halves back together again to form 8 jalapeños. 3. Season the ground beef with the pepper and salt and mix with your hands to incorporate. Flatten about ¼ pound of ground beef in the palm of your hand and place a stuffed jalapeño in the center. Fold the beef around the jalapeño, forming an egg shape. Wrap the beef-covered jalapeño with a slice of bacon and secure it with a toothpick. 4. Place the jalapeños on the Baking Pan, leaving space between them and working in batches if necessary, and slide the Pan into shelf position 4/5. 5. Select the Bacon setting. Set the cooking temperature to 400°F/204°C and the cooking time to 15 minutes. Cook until the beef is cooked through and the bacon is crispy. Garnish with cilantro before serving. 6. Store leftovers in an airtight container in the fridge for 3 days or in the freezer for up to a month. Reheat in the Air Fryer at 350°F/176°C for 4 minutes, or until heated through and the bacon is crispy.

Quick Carne Asada

Prep Time: 5 minutes | Cook Time: 8 minutes | Serves: 4

Marinade:

1 cup fresh cilantro leaves and stems, plus more for garnish if desired	1 teaspoon stevia glycerite, or ⅛ teaspoon liquid stevia
1 jalapeño pepper, seeded and diced	2 teaspoons ancho chili powder
½ cup lime juice	2 teaspoons fine sea salt
2 tablespoons avocado oil	1 teaspoon coriander seeds
2 tablespoons coconut vinegar or apple cider vinegar	1 teaspoon cumin seeds
2 teaspoons orange extract	1 pound skirt steak, cut into 4 equal portions

For Serving (Optional):

Chopped avocado	Sliced radishes
Lime slices	

1. Make the marinade by placing all the ingredients for the marinade in a blender and puree until smooth. 2. Add the steak to a shallow dish and pour the marinade over it, making sure the meat is covered completely. Cover and place in the fridge for 2 hours or overnight. 3. Spray the Wire Rack with avocado oil. 4. Remove the steak from the marinade and place it on Wire Rack in one layer. Slide the Wire Rack into shelf position 2 with the Baking Pan placed underneath. 5. Select the Steak setting. Set the cooking temperature to 400°F/204°C and the cooking time to 8 minutes. Cook until the internal temperature is 145°F; do not overcook or it will become tough. 6. Remove the steak and place it on a cutting board to rest for 10 minutes before slicing it against the grain. Garnish with the cilantro, if desired, and serve with the chopped avocado, lime slices, and/or sliced radishes, if desired. 7. Store leftovers in an airtight container in the fridge for 3 days or in the freezer for up to a month. Reheat in the Air Fryer at 350°F/176°C for 4 minutes, or until heated through.

Quick Pigs in a Blanket

Prep Time: 10 minutes | Cook Time: 7 minutes | Serves: 2

½ cup shredded mozzarella cheese	2 (2-ounce) beef smoked sausages
2 tablespoons blanched finely ground almond flour	½ teaspoon sesame seeds
1 ounce full-fat cream cheese	

1. Place almond flour, mozzarella, and cream cheese in a large microwave-safe bowl. Microwave for 45 seconds and stir until smooth. Roll dough into a ball and cut in half. 2. Press each half out into a 4" × 5" rectangle. Roll one sausage up in each dough half and press seams closed. Sprinkle the top with sesame seeds. 3. Place each wrapped sausage on the Crisper Tray and slide the Crisper Tray into shelf position 4/5. 4. Select the Air Fry setting. Set the cooking temperature to 400°F/204°C and the cooking time to 7 minutes. 5. The outside will be golden when completely cooked. Serve immediately.

Healthy Fajita Meatball Lettuce Wraps

Prep Time: 10 minutes | Cook Time: 10 minutes | Serves: 4

1 pound ground beef (85% lean)	1 teaspoon fine sea salt
½ cup salsa, plus more for serving if desired	½ teaspoon chili powder
¼ cup chopped onions	½ teaspoon ground cumin
¼ cup diced green or red bell peppers	1 clove garlic, minced
1 large egg, beaten	
For Serving (Optional):	
8 leaves Boston lettuce	Lime slices
Pico de gallo or salsa	

1. Spray the Crisper Tray with avocado oil. 2. In a large bowl, mix up all the ingredients until well combined. 3. Shape the meat mixture into eight 1-inch balls. Place the meatballs on the Crisper Tray, leaving a little space between them, and slide the Tray into shelf position 4/5. 4. Select the Air Fry setting. Set the cooking temperature to 350°F/176°C and the cooking time to 10 minutes. Cook until cooked through and no longer pink inside and the internal temperature reaches 145°F. 5. Serve each meatball on a lettuce leaf, topped with pico de gallo or salsa, if desired. Serve with lime slices if desired. 6. Store leftovers in an airtight container in the fridge for 3 days or in the freezer for up to a month. Reheat in the Air Fryer at 350°F/176°C for 4 minutes, or until heated through.

Flavorful Cheeseburger Meatballs

Prep Time: 10 minutes | Cook Time: 16 minutes | Serves: 4

1 pound ground beef	½ teaspoon garlic powder
¼ cup diced onions	½ teaspoon ground black pepper
1 large egg	1 cup mushrooms (about 8 ounces), finely chopped
1½ teaspoons smoked paprika	½ cup tomato sauce
½ teaspoon fine sea salt	1 dozen (½-inch) cubes cheddar cheese
For Serving (Optional):	
Prepared yellow mustard	Sugar-free or reduced-sugar ketchup

1. Spray the Crisper Tray with avocado oil. 2. In a large bowl, mix together the ground beef, onions, salt, garlic powder, egg, paprika, and pepper until well combined. Add the mushrooms and slowly stir in the tomato sauce. The mixture should be very moist but still hold its shape when rolled into meatballs. 3. Divide the mixture into 12 equal portions. Place 1 cube of cheese in the center of each portion and form the meat around the cheese into a 2-inch meatball. Arrange the meatballs in a single layer on the Crisper Tray, leaving a little space between them, and slide the Tray into shelf position 4/5. 4. Select the Air Fry setting. Set the cooking temperature to 375°F/190°C and the cooking time to 8 minutes. 5. Then flip them over and lower the temperature to 325°F/163°C. Cook for another 6 to 8 minutes, until cooked through. 6. Serve with mustard and ketchup, if desired. Store leftovers in an airtight container in the refrigerator for up to 4 days or in the freezer for up to 2 months. Reheat in the Air Fryer at 350°F/176°C for about 3 minutes, until heated through.

Homemade Mozzarella–Stuffed Meatloaf

Prep Time: 10 minutes | Cook Time: 30 minutes | Serves: 6

1 pound 80/20 ground beef	¼ teaspoon ground black pepper
½ medium green bell pepper, seeded and chopped	2 ounces mozzarella cheese, sliced into ¼"-thick slices
¼ medium yellow onion, peeled and chopped	¼ cup low-carb ketchup
½ teaspoon salt	

1. In a large bowl, combine onion, ground beef, salt, bell pepper, and black pepper. Cut a piece of parchment to fit the Crisper Tray. Place half beef mixture on ungreased parchment and form a 9" × 4" loaf, about ½" thick. 2. Center mozzarella slices on beef loaf, leaving at least ¼" around each edge. 3. Press remaining beef into a second 9" × 4" loaf and place on top of mozzarella, pressing edges of loaves together to seal. 4. Place parchment with meatloaf into the Crisper Tray and slide the Tray into shelf position 4/5. Select the Air Fry setting. Set the cooking temperature to 350°F/176°C and the cooking time to 30 minutes. 5. Carefully turn the loaf and brushing top with ketchup halfway through cooking. 6. Loaf will be browned and have an internal temperature of at least 180°F when done. Slice and serve warm.

Juicy Marinated Steak Kebabs

Prep Time: 45 minutes | Cook Time: 5 minutes | Serves: 4

1 pound strip steak, fat trimmed, cut into 1" cubes	½ teaspoon salt
½ cup soy sauce	¼ teaspoon ground black pepper
¼ cup olive oil	1 medium green bell pepper, seeded and chopped into 1" cubes
1 tablespoon granular brown erythritol	

1. Place steak into a large sealable bowl or bag and pour in soy sauce and olive oil. Add erythritol and stir to coat steak. Marinate at room temperature 30 minutes. 2. Remove streak from marinade and sprinkle with black pepper and salt. 3. Place meat and vegetables onto 6" skewer sticks, alternating between steak and bell pepper. 4. Place kebabs on the Crisper Tray and slide the Tray into shelf position 4/5 with the Baking Pan placed underneath to catch the drippings. 5. Select the Air Fry setting. Set the cooking temperature to 400°F/204°C and the cooking time to 5 minutes. 6. Steak will be done when crispy at the edges and peppers are tender. Serve warm.

Chapter 6 Seafood

Easy Bacon-Wrapped Scallops

Prep Time: 5 minutes | Cook Time: 10 minutes | Serves: 4

8 (1-ounce) sea scallops, cleaned and patted dry	¼ teaspoon salt
8 slices sugar-free bacon	¼ teaspoon ground black pepper

1. Wrap each scallop in 1 slice bacon and secure with a toothpick. Sprinkle with salt and pepper. 2. Place scallops on the Baking Pan and slide the Baking Pan into shelf position 4/5. 3. Select the Bacon setting. Set the cooking temperature to 360°F/182°C and the cooking time to 10 minutes. 4. Scallops will be opaque and firm, and have an internal temperature of 130°F when done. Serve warm.

Cajun Popcorn Shrimp

Prep Time: 10 minutes | Cook Time: 9 minutes | Serves: 4

4 large egg yolks	½ cup finely shredded Gouda or Parmesan cheese
1 teaspoon prepared yellow mustard	½ cup pork dust
1 pound small shrimp, peeled, deveined, and tails removed	1 tablespoon Cajun seasoning
For Serving/Garnish (Optional):	
Prepared yellow mustard	Tomato sauce
Ranch Dressing	Sprig of fresh parsley

1. Spray the Crisper Tray with avocado oil. 2. Add the egg yolks to a large bowl, place in the mustard, and whisk until well combined. Add the shrimp and stir well to coat. 3. In a medium-sized bowl, mix up the cheese, pork dust, and Cajun seasoning until well combined. 4. One at a time, roll the coated shrimp in the pork dust mixture and use your hands to press it onto the shrimp. Spray the coated shrimp with avocado oil and place them on the Crisper Tray, leaving space between them, and slide the Crisper Tray into shelf position 4/5. 5. Select the Air Fry setting. Set the cooking temperature to 400°F/204°C and the cooking time to 9 minutes. Cook the shrimp until cooked through and no longer translucent, flipping after 4 minutes. 6. Serve with your dipping sauces of choice and garnish with a sprig of fresh parsley. Store leftovers in an airtight container in the refrigerator for up to 3 days. Reheat in the air fryer at 400°F/204°C for 5 minutes, or until warmed through.

Crispy BLT Crab Cakes

Prep Time: 10 minutes | Cook Time: 19 minutes | Serves: 4

4 slices bacon	
Crab Cakes:	
1 pound canned lump crabmeat, drained well	½ teaspoon dried parsley
¼ cup plus 1 tablespoon powdered Parmesan cheese (or pork dust for dairy-free)	½ teaspoon dried dill weed
	¼ teaspoon garlic powder
3 tablespoons mayonnaise	¼ teaspoon onion powder
1 large egg	⅛ teaspoon ground black pepper
½ teaspoon dried chives	1 cup pork dust
For Serving:	
Leaves from 1 small head Boston lettuce	¼ cup mayonnaise
4 slices tomato	

1. Spray the Baking Pan with avocado oil. 2. Place the bacon slices on the Baking Pan, leaving space between them, and slide the Baking Pan into shelf position 4/5. Select the Bacon setting. Set the cooking temperature to 350°F/176°C and the cooking time to 9 minutes. Cook until crispy. Remove the bacon and set the bacon aside. 3. Make the crab cakes by placing all the crab cake ingredients except the pork dust in a large bowl and mix together with your hands until well blended. Divide the mixture into 4 equal-sized crab cakes that are about 1 inch thick. 4. Place the pork dust in a small bowl. Dredge the crab cakes in the pork dust to coat them well and use your hands to press the pork dust into the cakes. 5. Place the crab cakes on the Crisper Tray, leaving space between them, and slide the Crisper Tray into shelf position 4/5. Select the Air Fry setting. Set the cooking temperature to 400°F/204°C and the cooking time to 10 minutes. Cook until crispy on the outside. 6. To serve, place 4 lettuce leaves on a serving platter and top each leaf with a slice of tomato, then a crab cake, then a dollop of mayo, and finally a slice of bacon. 7. Store leftovers in an airtight container in the refrigerator for up to 3 days. Reheat in the air fryer at 350°F/176°C for 6 minutes, or until heated through.

Spicy Cilantro Lime Baked Salmon

Prep Time: 10 minutes | Cook Time: 12 minutes | Serves: 2

2 (3-ounce) salmon fillets, skin removed
1 tablespoon salted butter, melted
1 teaspoon chili powder
½ teaspoon finely minced garlic

¼ cup sliced pickled jalapeños
½ medium lime, juiced
2 tablespoons chopped cilantro

1 Place salmon fillets the Baking Pan. Brush each with butter and sprinkle with chili powder and garlic. 2. Place jalapeño slices on top and around salmon. Pour half of the lime juice over the salmon and cover with foil. Slide the Baking Pan into shelf position 4/5. 3. Select the Bake setting. Set the cooking temperature to 370°F/187°C and the cooking time to 12 minutes. 4. When fully cooked, salmon should flake easily with a fork and reach an internal temperature of at least 145°F. 5. To serve, spritz with remaining lime juice and garnish with cilantro.

Healthy Rainbow Salmon Kebabs

Prep Time: 10 minutes | Cook Time: 8 minutes | Serves: 2

6 ounces boneless, skinless salmon, cut into 1" cubes
¼ medium red onion, peeled and cut into 1" pieces
½ medium yellow bell pepper, seeded and cut into 1" pieces
½ medium zucchini, trimmed and cut into ½" slices

1 tablespoon olive oil
½ teaspoon salt
¼ teaspoon ground black pepper

1. Using one 6" skewer, skewer 1 piece salmon, then 1 piece onion, 1 piece bell pepper, and finally 1 piece zucchini. Repeat this pattern with additional skewers to make four kebabs total. Drizzle with the olive oil and sprinkle with the black pepper and salt. 2. Place kebabs on the Crisper Tray and slide the Crisper Tray into shelf position 4/5. Select the Air Fry setting. Set the cooking temperature to 400°F/204°C and the cooking time to 8 minutes. Turn kebabs halfway through cooking. 3. Salmon will easily flake and have an internal temperature of at least 145°F when done; vegetables will be tender. Serve warm.

Pesto Parmesan–Crusted Shrimp Zoodles

Prep Time: 10 minutes | Cook Time: 7 minutes | Serves: 4

2 large eggs
3 cloves garlic, minced
2 teaspoons dried basil, divided
½ teaspoon fine sea salt
Pesto:
1 packed cup fresh basil
¼ cup extra-virgin olive oil or avocado oil
¼ cup grated Parmesan cheese
¼ cup roasted, salted walnuts (omit for nut-free)
3 cloves garlic, peeled

½ teaspoon ground black pepper
½ cup powdered Parmesan cheese (about 1½ ounces)
1 pound jumbo shrimp, peeled, deveined, butterflied, tails removed

1 tablespoon lemon juice
½ teaspoon fine sea salt
¼ teaspoon ground black pepper
2 recipes Perfect Zoodles, warm, for serving

1. Spray the Crisper Tray with avocado oil. 2. In a large bowl, whisk together the eggs, garlic, 1 teaspoon of the dried basil, the salt, and the pepper. In a separate small bowl, mix together the remaining teaspoon of dried basil and the Parmesan cheese. 3. Place the shrimp in the bowl with the egg mixture and use your hands to coat the shrimp. Roll one shrimp in the Parmesan mixture and press the coating onto the shrimp with your hands. Working in batches if necessary, place the coated shrimp on the Crisper Tray. Repeat with the remaining shrimp, leaving space between them on the Crisper Tray. Slide the Crisper Tray into shelf position 4/5. 4. Select the Air Fry setting. Set the cooking temperature to 400°F/204°C and the cooking time to 18 minutes. Cook the shrimp until cooked through and no longer translucent, flipping after 4 minutes. 5. While the shrimp cook, make the pesto by placing all the ingredients for the pesto in a food processor and pulse until smooth, with a few rough pieces of basil. 6. Just before serving, toss the warm zoodles with the pesto and place the shrimp on top. 7. Store leftover shrimp and pesto zoodles in separate airtight containers in the refrigerator for up to 3 days or in the freezer for up to a month. Reheat the shrimp in the air fryer at 350°F/176°C for 5 minutes, or until warmed through. To reheat the pesto zoodles, place them in a casserole dish that will fits in the appliance and cook at 350°F/176°C for 2 minutes, or until heated through.

Lemony Butter Lobster Tails

Prep Time: 5 minutes | Cook Time: 9 minutes | Serves: 4

4 (6-ounce) lobster tails
2 tablespoons salted butter, melted
1 tablespoon peeled and finely minced garlic

¼ teaspoon salt
¼ teaspoon ground black pepper
2 tablespoons lemon juice

1. Carefully cut open lobster tails with scissors and pull back shell a little to expose meat. Pour butter over each tail and then sprinkle with salt, garlic, and pepper. 2. Place tails on the Crisper Tray and slide the Crisper Tray into shelf position 4/5. Select the Air Fry setting. Set the cooking temperature to 400°F/204°C and the cooking time to 9 minutes. Lobster will be firm and opaque when done. 3. Transfer tails to four medium plates and pour lemon juice over lobster meat. Serve warm.

Homemade Breaded Shrimp Tacos

Prep Time: 10 minutes | Cook Time: 9 minutes | Serves: 4

2 large eggs
1 teaspoon prepared yellow mustard
1 pound small shrimp, peeled, deveined, and tails removed
For Serving:
8 large Boston lettuce leaves
¼ cup pico de gallo
¼ cup shredded purple cabbage

½ cup finely shredded Gouda or Parmesan cheese
½ cup pork dust

1 lemon, sliced
Guacamole (optional)

1. Crack the eggs into a large bowl, place in the mustard, and whisk until well combined. Add the shrimp and stir well to coat. 2. In a medium-sized bowl, mix up the cheese and pork dust until well combined. 3. One at a time, roll the coated shrimp in the pork dust mixture and use your hands to press it onto each shrimp. 4. Spray the coated shrimp with avocado oil and place them on the Crisper Tray, leaving space between them, and slide the Crisper Tray into shelf position 4/5. 5. Select the Air Fry setting. Set the cooking temperature to 400°F/204°C and the cooking time to 9 minutes. 5. Cook the shrimp until cooked through and no longer translucent, flipping after 4 minutes. 6. To serve, place a lettuce leaf on a serving plate, place several shrimp on top, and top with 1½ teaspoons each of pico de gallo and purple cabbage. Squeeze some lemon juice on top and serve with guacamole, if desired. 7. Store leftover shrimp in an airtight container in the refrigerator for up to 3 days. Reheat in the air fryer at 400°F/204°C for 5 minutes, or until warmed through.

Delicious Cod over Creamy Leek Noodles

Prep Time: 10 minutes | Cook Time: 24 minutes | Serves: 4

1 small leek, sliced into long thin noodles (about 2 cups)
½ cup heavy cream
2 cloves garlic, minced
Coating:
¼ cup grated Parmesan cheese
2 tablespoons mayonnaise
2 tablespoons unsalted butter, softened

1 teaspoon fine sea salt, divided
4 (4-ounce) cod fillets (about 1 inch thick)
½ teaspoon ground black pepper

1 tablespoon chopped fresh thyme, or ½ teaspoon dried thyme leaves, plus more for garnish

1. Place the leek noodles in a 6-inch casserole dish or a pan that fits in the appliance. 2. In a small bowl, stir together the cream, garlic, and ½ teaspoon of the salt. Pour the mixture over the leeks. 3. Slide the Crisper Tray with the dish on top into shelf position 4/5. Select the Air Fry setting. Set the cooking temperature to 350°F/176°C and the cooking time to 10 minutes. Cook until the leeks are very tender. 4. Pat the fish dry and season with the pepper and the remaining ½ teaspoon of salt. When the leeks are ready, open and place the fish fillets on top of the leeks. Cook for 8 to 10 minutes, until the fish flakes easily with a fork. 5. While the fish cooks, make the coating by combining the Parmesan, mayo, butter, and thyme in a small bowl. 6. When the fish is ready, remove from the dish and spread with a ½-inch-thick to ¾-inch-thick layer of the coating. 7. Place the fish back in the dish and cook at 425°F/218°C for 3 to 4 minutes, until the coating browns. 8. Garnish with fresh or dried thyme, if desired. Store leftovers in an airtight container in the refrigerator for up to 3 days. Reheat in a casserole dish in the air fryer at 350°F/176°C for 6 minutes, or until heated through.

Mayo Fish Taco Bowl

Prep Time: 10 minutes | Cook Time: 12 minutes | Serves: 4

½ teaspoon salt	4 cups finely shredded green cabbage
¼ teaspoon garlic powder	⅓ cup mayonnaise
¼ teaspoon ground cumin	¼ teaspoon ground black pepper
4 (4-ounce) cod fillets	¼ cup chopped pickled jalapeños

1. Sprinkle salt, garlic powder, and cumin over cod and place on the Crisper Tray and slide the Crisper Tray into shelf position 4/5. 2. Select the Air Fry setting. Set the cooking temperature to 350°F/176°C and the cooking time to 12 minutes. Turn fillets halfway through cooking. 3. Cod will flake easily and have an internal temperature of at least 145°F when done. 4. In a large bowl, toss cabbage with mayonnaise, pepper, and jalapeños until fully coated. Serve cod warm over cabbage slaw on four medium plates.

Simple Asian Marinated Salmon

Prep Time: 5 minutes | Cook Time: 6 minutes | Serves: 2

Marinade:

¼ cup wheat-free tamari or coconut aminos	2 teaspoons grated fresh ginger
2 tablespoons lime or lemon juice	2 cloves garlic, minced
2 tablespoons sesame oil	½ teaspoon ground black pepper
2 tablespoons Swerve confectioners'-style sweetener, or a few drops liquid stevia	2 (4-ounce) salmon fillets (about 1¼ inches thick)
	Sliced green onions, for garnish

Sauce (Optional):

¼ cup beef broth	1 tablespoon tomato sauce
¼ cup wheat-free tamari	1 teaspoon stevia glycerite (optional)
3 tablespoons Swerve confectioners'-style sweetener or equivalent amount of liquid or powdered sweetener	⅛ teaspoon guar gum or xanthan gum (optional, for thickening)

1. Make the marinade by placing all the ingredients for the marinade in a medium-sized shallow dish and stir together until well combined. Place the salmon in the marinade. Cover and refrigerate for at least 2 hours or overnight. 2. Take the salmon fillets out of the marinade and place them on the Baking Pan, leaving space between them, and slide the Baking Pan into shelf position 2. 3. Select the Fish setting. Set the cooking temperature to 400°F/204°C and the cooking time to 6 minutes. Cook until the salmon is cooked through and flakes easily with a fork. 4. While the salmon cooks, make the sauce by placing all the sauce ingredients, if using, except the guar gum in a medium-sized bowl and stir until well combined. Taste and adjust the sweetness to your liking. While whisking slowly, add the guar gum. Let the sauce thicken for 3 to 5 minutes. Drizzle the sauce on top of the salmon before serving. 5. Garnish the salmon with sliced green onions before serving. Store leftovers in an airtight container in the fridge for up to 3 days. The sauce can be made up to 3 days ahead and stored in an airtight container in the fridge. Reheat in the air fryer at 350°F/176°C for 3 minutes, or until heated through.

Southern Air-Fried Catfish

Prep Time: 10 minutes | Cook Time: 12 minutes | Serves: 4

4 (7-ounce) catfish fillets	2 teaspoons Old Bay Seasoning
⅓ cup heavy whipping cream	½ teaspoon salt
1 tablespoon lemon juice	¼ teaspoon ground black pepper
1 cup blanched finely ground almond flour	

1. Place catfish fillets into a large bowl with cream and pour in lemon juice. Stir to coat. 2. In a separate large bowl, combine flour and Old Bay Seasoning. 3. Remove each fillet and gently shake off excess cream. Sprinkle with salt and pepper. Press each fillet gently into flour mixture on both sides to coat. 4. Place fillets on the Crisper Tray and slide the Crisper Tray into shelf position 4/5. Select the Air Fry setting. Set the cooking temperature to 400°F/204°C and the cooking time to 12 minutes. Turn the fillets halfway through cooking. 5. Catfish will be golden brown and have an internal temperature of at least 145°F when done. Serve warm.

Refreshing Lemon Garlic Scallops

Prep Time: 5 minutes | Cook Time: 10 minutes | Serves: 4

4 tablespoons salted butter, melted	8 (1-ounce) sea scallops, cleaned and patted dry
4 teaspoons peeled and finely minced garlic	¼ teaspoon salt
½ small lemon, zested and juiced	¼ teaspoon ground black pepper

1. In a small bowl, mix up butter, lemon zest, and lemon juice. Place scallops on the Baking Pan. Pour butter mixture over scallops and then sprinkle with salt and pepper. 2. Slide the Baking Pan into shelf position 4/5. Select the Air Fry setting. Set the cooking temperature to 360°F/182°C and the cooking time to 10 minutes. 3. Scallops will be opaque and firm, and have an internal temperature of 130°F when done. Serve warm.

Crispy Tuna Melt Croquettes

Prep Time: 10 minutes | Cook Time: 8 minutes | Serves: 6

2 (5-ounce) cans tuna, drained	2 teaspoons prepared yellow mustard
1 (8-ounce) package cream cheese, softened	1 large egg
½ cup finely shredded cheddar cheese	1½ cups pork dust or powdered Parmesan cheese
2 tablespoons diced onions	Fresh dill, for garnish (optional)
For Serving (Optional):	
Cherry tomatoes	Prepared yellow mustard
Mayonnaise	

1. In a large bowl, stir together the tuna, cheddar cheese, cream cheese, onions, mustard, and egg until well combined. 2. Place the pork dust in a shallow bowl. 3. Form the tuna mixture into twelve 1½-inch balls. Roll the balls in the pork dust and press it into a thick crust around each ball with your hands. Flatten the balls into ½-inch-thick patties. 4. Working in batches to avoid overcrowding, place the patties on the Crisper Tray, leaving space between them, and slide the Crisper Tray into shelf position 4/5. Select the Air Fry setting. Set the cooking temperature to 400°F/204°C and the cooking time to 8 minutes. Cook until golden brown and crispy, flipping the patties halfway through. 5. Garnish the croquettes with fresh dill, if desired, and serve with cherry tomatoes and dollops of mayo and mustard on the side. 6. Store leftovers in an airtight container in the refrigerator for up to 4 days. Reheat in the Air Fryer at 400°F/204°C for about 3 minutes, until heated through.

Crispy Almond Pesto Salmon

Prep Time: 5 minutes | Cook Time: 12 minutes | Serves: 2

¼ cup pesto	2 (1½"-thick) salmon fillets (about 4 ounces each)
¼ cup sliced almonds, roughly chopped	2 tablespoons unsalted butter, melted

1. In a small bowl, mix pesto and almonds. Set aside. 2. Place fillets on the Baking Pan. 3. Brush each fillet with butter and place half of the pesto mixture on the top of each fillet. Slide the Baking Pan into shelf position 4/5. 4. Select the Air Fry setting. Set the cooking temperature to 390°F/198°C and the cooking time to 12 minutes. 5. Salmon will easily flake when fully cooked and reach an internal temperature of at least 145°F. Serve warm.

Healthy Tuna Cakes

Prep Time: 10 minutes | Cook Time: 10 minutes | Serves: 4

4 (3-ounce) pouches tuna, drained	2 tablespoons peeled and chopped white onion
1 large egg, whisked	½ teaspoon Old Bay Seasoning

1. In a large bowl, combine all ingredients together and form into four patties. 2. Place patties on the Crisper Tray and slide the Crisper Tray into shelf position 4/5. Select the Air Fry setting. Set the cooking temperature to 400°F/204°C and the cooking time to 10 minutes. 3. Patties will be browned and crispy when done. Let cool 5 minutes before serving.

Old Bay Crab Cakes

Prep Time: 10 minutes | Cook Time: 10 minutes | Serves: 4

2 (6-ounce) cans lump crabmeat
¼ cup blanched finely ground almond flour
1 large egg
2 tablespoons full-fat mayonnaise
½ teaspoon Dijon mustard

½ tablespoon lemon juice
½ medium green bell pepper, seeded and chopped
¼ cup chopped green onion
½ teaspoon Old Bay seasoning

1. In a large bowl, mix up all ingredients. Form into four balls and flatten into patties. Place patties on the Crisper Tray and slide the Crisper Tray into shelf position 4/5. 2. Select the Air Fry setting. Set the cooking temperature to 350°F/176°C and the cooking time to 10 minutes. 3. Flip the patties halfway through the cooking time. Serve warm.

Tasty Sesame–Crusted Tuna Steak

Prep Time: 5 minutes | Cook Time: 8 minutes | Serves: 2

2 (6-ounce) tuna steaks
1 tablespoon coconut oil, melted
½ teaspoon garlic powder

2 teaspoons white sesame seeds
2 teaspoons black sesame seeds

1. Brush each tuna steak with coconut oil and sprinkle with garlic powder. 2. In a large bowl, mix sesame seeds and then press each tuna steak into them, covering the steak as completely as possible. Place tuna steaks on the Crisper Tray and slide the Crisper Tray into shelf position 4/5. 3. Select the Air Fry setting. Set the cooking temperature to 400°F/204°C and the cooking time to 8 minutes. 4. Flip the steaks halfway through the cooking time. Steaks will be well-done at 145°F internal temperature. Serve warm.

Mayo Crab–Stuffed Avocado Boats

Prep Time: 5 minutes | Cook Time: 7 minutes | Serves: 4

2 medium avocados, halved and pitted
8 ounces cooked crabmeat
¼ teaspoon Old Bay Seasoning

2 tablespoons peeled and diced yellow onion
2 tablespoons mayonnaise

1. Scoop out avocado flesh in each avocado half, leaving ½" around edges to form a shell. Chop scooped-out avocado. 2. In a medium bowl, combine crabmeat, onion, mayonnaise, Old Bay Seasoning, and chopped avocado. Place ¼ mixture into each avocado shell. 3. Place avocado boats on the Crisper Tray and slide the Crisper Tray into shelf position 4/5. Select the Air Fry setting. Set the cooking temperature to 350°F/176°C and the cooking time to 7 minutes. 4. Avocado will be browned on the top and mixture will be bubbling when done. Serve warm.

Italian Baked Cod Fillets

Prep Time: 5 minutes | Cook Time: 12 minutes | Serves: 4

4 (6-ounce) cod fillets
2 tablespoons salted butter, melted
1 teaspoon Italian seasoning

¼ teaspoon salt
½ cup low-carb marinara sauce

1. Place cod into on the Baking Pan. Pour butter over cod and sprinkle with Italian seasoning and salt. Top with marinara. 2. Slide the Pan into shelf position 2. Select the Fish setting. Set the cooking temperature to 350°F/176°C and the cooking time to 12 minutes. 3. Fillets will be lightly browned, easily flake, and have an internal temperature of at least 145°F when done. Serve warm.

Lemony Cod with Cherry Tomatoes and Olives

Prep Time: 5 minutes | Cook Time: 12 minutes | Serves: 4

4 (6-ounce) cod fillets	¼ teaspoon salt
3 tablespoons fresh lemon juice	6 cherry tomatoes, halved
1 tablespoon olive oil	¼ cup pitted and sliced kalamata olives

1. Place cod on the Baking Pan. Pour lemon juice into dish and drizzle cod with olive oil. Sprinkle with salt. Place tomatoes and olives around the Baking Pan in between fillets. 2. Slide the Baking Pan into shelf position 4/5. Select the Fish setting. Set the cooking temperature to 350°F/176°C and the cooking time to 12 minutes. Carefully turn cod halfway through cooking. 3. Fillets will be lightly browned, easily flake, and have an internal temperature of at least 145°F when done. Serve warm.

Paprika Salmon Fillets

Prep Time: 5 minutes | Cook Time: 7 minutes | Serves: 2

2 (4-ounce) boneless, skinless salmon fillets	½ teaspoon garlic powder
2 tablespoons salted butter, softened	1 teaspoon paprika
⅛ teaspoon cayenne pepper	¼ teaspoon ground black pepper

1. Brush both sides of each fillet with butter. In a small bowl, mix up the remaining ingredients and rub into fish on both sides. 2. Place fillets on the Crisper Tray and slide the Crisper Tray into shelf position 4/5. Select the Air Fry setting. Set the cooking temperature to 390°F/198°C and the cooking time to 7 minutes. 3. Internal temperature will be 145°F when done. Serve warm.

Maple Buttered Salmon Fillets

Prep Time: 5 minutes | Cook Time: 12 minutes | Serves: 4

2 tablespoons salted butter, melted	4 (4-ounce) boneless, skinless salmon fillets
1 teaspoon low-carb maple syrup	½ teaspoon salt
1 teaspoon yellow mustard	

1. In a small bowl, whisk together syrup, butter, and mustard. Brush ½ mixture over each fillet on both sides. Sprinkle fillets with salt on both sides. 2. Place salmon on the Baking Pan and slide the Baking Pan into shelf position 4/5. Select the Fish setting. Set the cooking temperature to 400°F/204°C and the cooking time to 12 minutes. Halfway through cooking, brush fillets on both sides with remaining syrup mixture. 3. Salmon will easily flake and have an internal temperature of at least 145°F when done. Serve warm.

Cajun Parmesan Lobster Tails

Prep Time: 5 minutes | Cook Time: 7 minutes | Serves: 4

4 (4-ounce) lobster tails	¼ teaspoon ground black pepper
2 tablespoons salted butter, melted	¼ cup grated Parmesan cheese
1½ teaspoons Cajun seasoning, divided	½ ounce plain pork rinds, finely crushed
¼ teaspoon salt	

1. Cut lobster tails open carefully with a pair of scissors and gently pull meat away from shells, resting meat on top of shells. 2. Brush lobster meat with butter and sprinkle with 1 teaspoon Cajun seasoning, ¼ teaspoon per tail. 3. In a small bowl, mix remaining Cajun seasoning, salt, Parmesan, pepper, and pork rinds. Gently press ¼ mixture onto meat on each lobster tail. 4. Carefully place tails on the Crisper Tray and slide the Crisper Tray into shelf position 4/5. Select the Air Fry setting. Set the cooking temperature to 400°F/204°C and the cooking time to 7 minutes. 5. Lobster tails will be crispy and golden on top and have an internal temperature of at least 145°F when done. Serve warm.

Crispy Mayo Crab Cakes

Prep Time: 10 minutes | Cook Time: 10 minutes | Serves: 4

8 ounces fresh lump crabmeat
2 tablespoons mayonnaise
1 teaspoon Old Bay Seasoning

½ ounce plain pork rinds, finely crushed
¼ cup seeded and chopped red bell pepper

1. In a large bowl, mix up all ingredients together. Separate into four equal sections and form into patties. 2. Slice a piece of parchment to fit the Crisper Tray and place it on the Crisper Tray. Place patties on the Crisper Tray and slide the Crisper Tray into shelf position 4/5. Select the Air Fry setting. Set the cooking temperature to 380°F/193°C and the cooking time to 18 minutes. Turn the patties halfway through cooking. 3. Crab cakes will be golden when done. Serve warm.

Snow Crab Legs with Lemony Butter

Prep Time: 5 minutes | Cook Time: 15 minutes | Serves: 4

8 pounds fresh shell-on snow crab legs
2 tablespoons coconut oil
2 teaspoons Old Bay Seasoning

4 tablespoons salted butter, melted
2 teaspoons lemon juice

1. Place crab legs on the Baking Pan, working in batches if needed. Drizzle legs with coconut oil and sprinkle with Old Bay Seasoning. Slide the Baking Pan into shelf position 4/5. 2. Select the Air Fry setting. Set the cooking temperature to 400°F/204°C and the cooking time to 15 minutes. Shake three times during cooking. 3. Legs will turn a bright red-orange when done. Serve warm. 4. In a separate small bowl, whisk butter and lemon juice for dipping. Serve on the side.

Easy Lemon Butter Cod

Prep Time: 5 minutes | Cook Time: 12 minutes | Serves: 4

4 (4-ounce) cod fillets
2 tablespoons salted butter, melted

1 teaspoon Old Bay Seasoning
½ medium lemon, cut into 4 slices

1. Place cod fillets on the Baking Pan. Brush tops of fillets with butter and sprinkle with Old Bay Seasoning. Lay 1 lemon slice on each fillet. 2. Cover the pan with aluminum foil and slide the Baking Pan into shelf position 4/5. Select the Fish setting. Set the cooking temperature to 350°F/176°C and the cooking time to 12 minutes. Turn the fillets halfway through cooking. 3. Fish will be opaque and have an internal temperature of at least 145°F when done. Serve warm.

Mayo Tuna–Stuffed Tomatoes

Prep Time: 5 minutes | Cook Time: 5 minutes | Serves: 2

2 medium beefsteak tomatoes, tops removed, seeded, membranes removed
2 (2.6-ounce) pouches tuna packed in water, drained
1 medium stalk celery, trimmed and chopped
2 tablespoons mayonnaise

¼ teaspoon salt
¼ teaspoon ground black pepper
2 teaspoons coconut oil
¼ cup shredded mild Cheddar cheese

1. Scoop pulp out of each tomato, leaving ½" shell. 2. In a medium bowl, mix tuna, celery, salt, mayonnaise, and pepper. Drizzle with coconut oil. Spoon ½ mixture into each tomato and top each with 2 tablespoons Cheddar. 3. Place tomatoes on the Crisper Tray and slide the Crisper Tray into shelf position 4/5. Select the Air Fry setting. Set the cooking temperature to 320°F/160°C and the cooking time to 5 minutes. 4. Cheese will be melted when done. Serve warm.

lemony Butter Crab Legs

Prep Time: 5 minutes | Cook Time: 15 minutes | Serves: 4

¼ cup salted butter, melted and divided
3 pounds crab legs

¼ teaspoon garlic powder
Juice of ½ medium lemon

1. In a large bowl, drizzle 2 tablespoons butter over crab legs. Place crab legs on the Crisper Tray and slide the Crisper Tray into shelf position 4/5. 2. Select the Air Fry setting. Set the cooking temperature to 400°F/204°C and the cooking time to 15 minutes. 3. Shake to toss the crab legs halfway through the cooking time. 4. In a small bowl, mix remaining butter, garlic powder, and lemon juice. 5. To serve, crack open crab legs and remove meat. Dip in lemon butter.

Flavorful Foil–Packet Lobster Tail

Prep Time: 15 minutes | Cook Time: 12 minutes | Serves: 2

2 (6-ounce) lobster tails, halved
2 tablespoons salted butter, melted
½ teaspoon Old Bay seasoning

Juice of ½ medium lemon
1 teaspoon dried parsley

1. Place the two halved tails on a sheet of aluminum foil. Drizzle with butter, Old Bay seasoning, and lemon juice. 2. Seal the foil packets, completely covering tails. Place on the Crisper Tray and slide the Crisper Tray into shelf position 4/5. 3. Select the Air Fry setting. Set the cooking temperature to 375°F/190°C and the cooking time to 12 minutes. 4. Once done, sprinkle with dried parsley and serve immediately.

Authentic Tuna Zoodle Casserole

Prep Time: 15 minutes | Cook Time: 15 minutes | Serves: 4

2 tablespoons salted butter
¼ cup diced white onion
¼ cup chopped white mushrooms
2 stalks celery, finely chopped
½ cup heavy cream
½ cup vegetable broth

2 tablespoons full-fat mayonnaise
¼ teaspoon xanthan gum
½ teaspoon red pepper flakes
2 medium zucchini, spiralized
2 (5-ounce) cans albacore tuna
1 ounce pork rinds, finely ground

1. In a large saucepan, melt butter over medium heat. Add onion, mushrooms, and celery and sauté until fragrant, about 3–5 minutes. 2. Pour in heavy cream, mayonnaise, vegetable broth, and xanthan gum. Reduce the heat and continue cooking for another 3 minutes, until the mixture begins to thicken. 3. Add red pepper flakes, zucchini, and tuna. Turn off heat and stir until zucchini noodles are coated. 4. Pour into 4-cup round baking dish that fits in the appliance. Top with ground pork rinds and cover the top of the dish with foil. Slide the Crisper Tray with the dish on top into shelf position 4/5. 5. Select the Air Fry setting. Set the cooking temperature to 370°F/187°C and the cooking time to 15 minutes. 6. When 3 minutes remain, remove the foil to brown the top of the casserole. Serve warm.

Mayo Salmon Patties

Prep Time: 5 minutes | Cook Time: 8 minutes | Serves: 4

12 ounces pouched pink salmon
3 tablespoons mayonnaise
⅓ cup blanched finely ground almond flour

½ teaspoon Cajun seasoning
1 medium avocado, peeled, pitted, and sliced

1. In a medium bowl, mix salmon, flour, mayonnaise, and Cajun seasoning. Form mixture into four patties. 2. Place patties on the Crisper Tray and slide the Crisper Tray into shelf position 4/5. Select the Air Fry setting. Set the cooking temperature to 400°F/204°C and the cooking time to 8 minutes. Turn the patties halfway through cooking. Patties will be done when firm and golden brown. 3. Transfer the patties to four medium plates and serve warm with avocado slices.

Classic Shrimp Scampi

Prep Time: 5 minutes | Cook Time: 8 minutes | Serves: 4

¼ cup unsalted butter (or butter-flavored coconut oil for dairy-free)	1 tablespoon chopped fresh parsley, plus more for garnish
2 tablespoons fish stock or chicken broth	1 teaspoon red pepper flakes
1 tablespoon lemon juice	1 pound large shrimp, peeled and deveined, tails removed
2 cloves garlic, minced	Fresh basil sprigs, for garnish
2 tablespoons chopped fresh basil leaves	

1. Place the butter, fish stock, lemon juice, garlic, basil, parsley, and red pepper flakes in the Baking Pan and stir to combine. 2. Slide the Baking Pan into shelf position 4/5. Select the Air Fry setting. Set the cooking temperature to 350°F/176°C and the cooking time to 3 minutes. Cook until fragrant and the garlic has softened. 3. Place in the shrimp and stir to coat the shrimp in the sauce. Cook for 5 minutes, or until the shrimp are pink, stirring after 3 minutes. Garnish with fresh basil sprigs and chopped parsley before serving. 4. Store leftovers in an airtight container in the refrigerator for up to 4 days. Reheat in the Air Fryer at 400°F/204°C for about 3 minutes, until heated through.

Simple Sea Scallops

Prep Time: 5 minutes | Cook Time: 4 minutes | Serves: 2

12 medium sea scallops	¾ teaspoon ground black pepper, plus more for garnish if desired
1 teaspoon fine sea salt	Fresh thyme leaves, for garnish (optional)

1. Spray the Crisper Tray with avocado oil. 2. Rinse the scallops and pat completely dry. Spray avocado oil on the scallops and season them with the pepper and salt. Place them on the Crisper Tray, spacing them apart and working in batches if necessary. Slide the Crisper Tray into shelf position 4/5. Select the Air Fry setting. Set the cooking temperature to 390°F/198°C and the cooking time to 2 minutes. Then flip the scallops and cook for an additional 2 minutes, or until cooked through and no longer translucent. Garnish with ground black pepper and thyme leaves, if desired. 3. Best served fresh. Store leftovers in an airtight container in the fridge for up to 3 days. Reheat in the Air Fryer at 350°F/176°C for 2 minutes, or until heated through.

Homemade Coconut Shrimp with Spicy Mayo

Prep Time: 10 minutes | Cook Time: 6 minutes | Serves: 4

1 pound large shrimp (about 2 dozen), peeled and deveined, tails on	1 tablespoon water
Fine sea salt and ground black pepper	½ cup unsweetened coconut flakes
2 large eggs	½ cup pork dust
Spicy Mayo:	
½ cup mayonnaise	½ teaspoon hot sauce
2 tablespoons beef or chicken broth	½ teaspoon cayenne pepper
For Serving (Optional):	
Microgreens	Thinly sliced radishes

1. Spray the Crisper Tray with avocado oil. 2. Season the shrimp well on all sides with pepper and salt. 3. Crack two eggs into a shallow baking dish, add the water and a pinch each of salt and pepper, and whisk to combine. In another shallow baking dish, stir the coconut flakes and pork dust until well combined. 4. Dip one shrimp in the eggs and let any excess egg drip off, then dredge both sides of the shrimp in the coconut mixture. Spray the shrimp with avocado oil and place it on the Crisper Tray. Repeat with the remaining shrimp, leaving space between them on the Crisper Tray. Slide the Crisper Tray into shelf position 4/5. 5. Select the Air Fry setting. Set the cooking temperature to 400°F/204°C and the cooking time to 6 minutes. Cook the shrimp until cooked through and no longer translucent, flipping halfway through. 6. While the shrimp cook, make the spicy mayo by adding all the spicy mayo ingredients in a medium-sized bowl and stir until well combined. 7. Serve the shrimp on a bed of microgreens and thinly sliced radishes, if desired. Serve the spicy mayo on the side for dipping. 8. Store leftovers in an airtight container in the refrigerator for up to 4 days. Reheat in the Air Fryer at 400°F/204°C for about 3 minutes, until heated through.

Crab Rangoon Patties with Sweet 'n' Sour Sauce

Prep Time: 10 minutes | Cook Time: 12 minutes | Serves: 8

Patties:

1 pound canned lump crabmeat, drained
1 (8-ounce) package cream cheese, softened
1 tablespoon chopped fresh chives

1 large egg
1 teaspoon grated fresh ginger
1 clove garlic, smashed to a paste or minced

Coating:

1½ cups pork dust

Dipping Sauce:

½ cup chicken broth
⅓ cup coconut aminos or wheat-free tamari
⅓ cup Swerve confectioners'-style sweetener or equivalent amount of liquid or powdered sweetener
¼ cup tomato sauce

1 tablespoon coconut vinegar or apple cider vinegar
¼ teaspoon grated fresh ginger
1 clove garlic, smashed to a paste
Sliced green onions, for garnish (optional)
Fried Cauliflower Rice, for serving (optional)

1. In a medium-sized bowl, gently mix all the ingredients for the patties, without breaking up the crabmeat. 2. Form the crab mixture into 8 2½ inches in diameter, ¾ inch thick patties. 3. Place the pork dust in a shallow dish. Place each patty in the pork dust and use your hands to press the pork dust into the patties to form a crust. Place the patties in a single layer on the Crisper Tray, leaving space between them and working in batches if necessary, and slide the Crisper Tray into shelf position 4/5. 4. Select the Air Fry setting. Set the cooking temperature to 400°F/204°C and the cooking time to 12 minutes. Cook until the crust is golden and crispy. 5. While the patties cook, make the dipping sauce by stir together all the sauce ingredients in a large saucepan. Bring to a simmer over medium-high heat, then turn the heat down to medium until the sauce has reduced and thickened, about 5 minutes. Taste and adjust the seasonings as desired. 6. Place the patties on a serving platter, drizzle with the dipping sauce, and garnish with sliced green onions, if desired. Serve the remaining dipping sauce on the side. Serve with fried cauliflower rice, if desired. 7. Store leftovers in an airtight container in the refrigerator for up to 3 days. Reheat the patties in the Air Fryer at 400°F/204°C for 4 minutes, or until crispy on the outside and heated through.

Crunchy Pecan–Crusted Catfish

Prep Time: 5 minutes | Cook Time: 12 minutes | Serves: 4

½ cup pecan meal
1 teaspoon fine sea salt

For Garnish (Optional):

Fresh oregano

¼ teaspoon ground black pepper
4 (4-ounce) catfish fillets

Pecan halves

1. Spray the Crisper Tray with avocado oil. 2. In a large bowl, mix the salt, pecan meal, and pepper. One at a time, dredge the catfish fillets in the mixture, coating them well and press the pecan meal into the fillets with your hands. Spray the fish with avocado oil and place them on the Crisper Tray and slide the Crisper Tray into shelf position 4/5. 3. Select the Air Fry setting. Set the cooking temperature to 375°F/190°C and the cooking time to 12 minutes. Cook the coated catfish until it flakes easily and is no longer translucent in the center, flipping halfway through. 4. Garnish with oregano sprigs and pecan halves, if desired. 5. Store leftovers in an airtight container in the fridge for up to 3 days. Reheat in the Air Fryer at 350°F/176°C for 4 minutes, or until heated through.

Delicious Friday Night Fish Fry

Prep Time: 10 minutes | Cook Time: 10 minutes | Serves: 4

1 large egg
½ cup powdered Parmesan cheese (about 1½ ounces) (or pork dust for dairy-free)
1 teaspoon smoked paprika
¼ teaspoon celery salt

¼ teaspoon ground black pepper
4 (4-ounce) cod fillets
Chopped fresh oregano or parsley, for garnish (optional)
Lemon slices, for serving (optional)

1. Spray the Crisper Tray with avocado oil. 2. Crack the egg in a shallow bowl and beat it lightly with a fork. Combine the Parmesan cheese, celery salt, paprika, and pepper in a separate shallow bowl. 3. One at a time, dip the fillets into the egg, then dredge them in the Parmesan mixture. Press the Parmesan onto the fillets to form a nice crust with your hands. As you finish, place the fish on the Crisper Tray and slide the Crisper Tray into shelf position 4/5. 4. Select the Air Fry setting. Set the cooking temperature to 400°F/204°C and the cooking time to 10 minutes. Cook the fish until cooked through and flakes easily with a fork. Garnish with the fresh oregano or parsley and serve with lemon slices, if desired. 5. Store leftovers in an airtight container in the refrigerator for up to 3 days. Reheat in the Air Fryer at 400°F/204°C for 5 minutes, or until warmed through.

Chapter 7 Desserts

Protein Doughnut Holes

Prep Time: 25 minutes | Cook Time: 6 minutes | Serves: 6

½ cup blanched finely ground almond flour	1 large egg
½ cup low-carb vanilla protein powder	5 tablespoons unsalted butter, melted
½ cup granular erythritol	½ teaspoon vanilla extract
½ teaspoon baking powder	

1. Mix up all ingredients in a large bowl. Place into the freezer for 20 minutes. 2. Wet your hands with water and roll the dough into twelve balls. 3. Cut a piece of parchment to the Crisper Tray. Working in batches as necessary, place doughnut holes on the Crisper Tray on top of parchment and slide the Crisper Tray into shelf position 4/5. 4. Select the Air Fry setting. Set the cooking temperature to 380°F/193°C and the cooking time to 6 minutes. 5. Flip doughnut holes halfway through the cooking time. 6. Let cool completely before serving.

Perfect Layered Peanut Butter Cheesecake Brownies

Prep Time: 20 minutes | Cook Time: 35 minutes | Serves: 6

½ cup blanched finely ground almond flour	2 large eggs, divided
1 cup powdered erythritol, divided	8 ounces full-fat cream cheese, softened
2 tablespoons unsweetened cocoa powder	¼ cup heavy whipping cream
½ teaspoon baking powder	1 teaspoon vanilla extract
¼ cup unsalted butter, softened	2 tablespoons no-sugar-added peanut butter

1. In a large bowl, mix together almond flour, ½ cup erythritol, cocoa powder, and baking powder. Stir in butter and one egg. 2. Scoop mixture into 6" round baking pan that fits in the appliance. Slide the Wire Rack into shelf position 6 and place the pan on the Wire Rack. 3. Select the Bake setting. Set the cooking temperature to 300°F/148°C and the cooking time to 20 minutes. 4. When fully cooked, a toothpick inserted in center will come out clean. Allow 20 minutes to fully cool and firm up. 5. In a large bowl, whisk cream cheese, remaining ½ cup erythritol, vanilla, heavy cream, peanut butter, and remaining egg until fluffy. 6. Pour mixture over cooled brownies. Place pan back into the appliance and cook at 300°F/148°C for 15 minutes. 7. Cheesecake will be slightly browned and mostly firm with a slight jiggle when done. Allow to cool, then refrigerate 2 hours before serving.

Pumpkin Roasted Spice Pecans

Prep Time: 5 minutes | Cook Time: 6 minutes | Serves: 4

1 cup whole pecans	½ teaspoon ground cinnamon
¼ cup granular erythritol	½ teaspoon pumpkin pie spice
1 large egg white	½ teaspoon vanilla extract

1. Combine all ingredients in a large bowl until pecans are coated. Place on the Crisper Tray and slide the Crisper Tray into shelf position 4/5. 2. Select the Air Fry setting. Set the cooking temperature to 300°F/148°C and the cooking time to 6 minutes. 3. Toss two to three times during cooking. 4. Allow to cool completely. Store in an airtight container up to 3 days.

Keto Coconut Flour Mug Cake

Prep Time: 5 minutes | Cook Time: 25 minutes | Serves: 1

1 large egg	2 tablespoons granular erythritol
2 tablespoons coconut flour	¼ teaspoon vanilla extract
2 tablespoons heavy whipping cream	¼ teaspoon baking powder

1. In a 4" ramekin, whisk egg, then add remaining ingredients. Stir until smooth. Place on the Crisper Tray and slide the Crisper Tray into shelf position 4/5. 2. Select the Air Fry setting. Set the cooking temperature to 300°F/148°C and the cooking time to 25 minutes. 3. When done, a toothpick should come out clean. Enjoy right out of the ramekin with a spoon. Serve warm.

Perfect Lemon Curd Pavlova

Prep Time: 10 minutes | Cook Time: 60 minutes | Serves: 4

Shell:

3 large egg whites

¼ teaspoon cream of tartar

¾ cup Swerve confectioners'-style sweetener or equivalent amount

of powdered sweetener

1 teaspoon grated lemon zest

1 teaspoon lemon extract

Lemon Curd:

1 cup Swerve confectioners'-style sweetener or equivalent amount of liquid or powdered sweetener

½ cup lemon juice

4 large eggs

½ cup coconut oil

For Garnish (Optional):

Blueberries

Swerve confectioners'-style sweetener or equivalent amount of

powdered sweetener

1. Thoroughly grease a 7-inch pie pan that fits in the appliance with butter or coconut oil. 2. Make the shell by using a hand mixer to beat the cream of tartar and egg whites in a small bowl until soft peaks form. With the mixer on low, slowly sprinkle in the sweetener and mix until it's completely incorporated. 3. Place in the lemon zest and lemon extract and continue to beat with the hand mixer until stiff peaks form. 4. Spoon the mixture into the greased pie pan, then smooth it across the bottom, up the sides, and onto the rim to form a shell. Slide the Wire Rack into shelf position 6 and place the pan on the Wire Rack. Select the Bake setting. Set the cooking temperature to 275°F/135°C and the cooking time to 60 minutes. Then turn off the appliance and let the shell stand in the appliance for 20 minutes. 5. While the shell bakes, make the lemon curd by adding the sweetener, lemon juice, and eggs in a medium-sized heavy-bottomed saucepan and whisk together. Add the coconut oil and place the pan on the stovetop over medium heat. Once the oil is melted, whisk constantly until the mixture thickens and thickly coats the back of a spoon, about 10 minutes. Do not allow the mixture to come to a boil. 6. Pour the lemon curd mixture through a fine-mesh strainer into a medium-sized bowl. Place the bowl inside a larger bowl filled with ice water and stir occasionally until the curd is completely cool, about 15 minutes. 7. Place the lemon curd on top of the shell and garnish with blueberries and powdered sweetener, if desired. Store leftovers in the refrigerator for up to 4 days.

Simple Toasted Coconut Flakes

Prep Time: 5 minutes | Cook Time: 3 minutes | Serves: 4

1 cup unsweetened coconut flakes

2 teaspoons coconut oil

¼ cup granular erythritol

⅛ teaspoon salt

1. Toss coconut flakes and oil in a large bowl until coated. Sprinkle with erythritol and salt. 2. Place coconut flakes on the Crisper Tray and slide the Crisper Tray into shelf position 4/5. 3. Select the Air Fry setting. Set the cooking temperature to 300°F/148°C and the cooking time to 3 minutes. 4. Toss the flakes when 1 minute remains. Add an extra minute if you would like a more golden coconut flake. 5. Store in an airtight container up to 3 days.

Baked Chocolate Meringue Cookies

Prep Time: 10 minutes | Cook Time: 60 minutes | Serves: 8

3 large egg whites

¼ teaspoon cream of tartar

¼ cup Swerve confectioners'-style sweetener or equivalent amount

of powdered sweetener

2 tablespoons unsweetened cocoa powder

1. Line a 7-inch pie pan or a dish that fits in the appliance with parchment paper. 2. In a small bowl, use a hand mixer to whip the egg whites and cream of tartar until soft peaks form. With the mixer on low, slowly sprinkle in the sweetener and mix until it's completely incorporated. Continue to beat with the mixer until stiff peaks form. 3. Add the cocoa powder and gently fold until it's completely combined. 4. Spoon the mixture into a piping bag with a ¾-inch tip. Pipe sixteen 1-inch meringue cookies onto the lined pie pan, spacing them about ¼ inch apart. 5. Slide the Wire Rack into shelf position 6 and place the pan on the Wire Rack. Select the Bake setting. Set the cooking temperature to 225°F/107°C and the cooking time to 60 minutes. Cook until the cookies are crispy on the outside, then turn off the appliance and let the cookies stand in the appliance for another 20 minutes before removing and serving.

Homemade Lemon Poppy Seed Macaroons

Prep Time: 10 minutes | Cook Time: 14 minutes | Serves: 6

2 large egg whites, room temperature	2 teaspoons poppy seeds
⅓ cup Swerve confectioners'-style sweetener or equivalent amount of powdered sweetener 2 tablespoons grated lemon zest, plus more for garnish if desired	1 teaspoon lemon extract
	¼ teaspoon fine sea salt
	2 cups unsweetened shredded coconut
Lemon Icing:	
¼ cup Swerve confectioners'-style sweetener or equivalent amount	of powdered sweetener 1 tablespoon lemon juice

1. Line a 7-inch pie pan or a casserole dish that fits in the appliance with parchment paper. 2. Add the egg whites to a medium-sized bowl and use a hand mixer on high to beat the whites until stiff peaks form. Add the sweetener, lemon zest, lemon extract, poppy seeds, and salt. Mix on low until combined. Use a rubber spatula to gently fold in the coconut. 3. Use a 1-inch cookie scoop to place the cookies on the parchment, spacing them about ¼ inch apart. Slide the Wire Rack into shelf position 6 and place the pan on the Wire Rack. Select the Bake setting. Set the cooking temperature to 325°F/163°C and the cooking time to 14 minutes. Cook for 12 to 14 minutes, until the cookies are golden and a toothpick inserted into the center comes out clean. 4. While the cookies bake, make the lemon icing by placing the sweetener in a small bowl. Add the lemon juice and stir well. If the icing is too thin, add a little more sweetener. If the icing is too thick, add a little more lemon juice. 5. Remove the cookies from the appliance and allow to cool for about 10 minutes, then drizzle with the icing. Garnish with lemon zest, if desired. 6. Store leftovers in an airtight container in the fridge for up to 5 days or in the freezer for up to a month.

Easy Roasted Pecan Clusters

Prep Time: 35 minutes | Cook Time: 8 minutes | Serves: 8

3 ounces whole shelled pecans	½ teaspoon ground cinnamon
1 tablespoon salted butter, melted	½ cup low-carb chocolate chips
2 teaspoons confectioners' erythritol	

1. In a medium bowl, toss pecans with butter and then sprinkle with erythritol and cinnamon. 2. Place pecans on the Crisper Tray and slide the Crisper Tray into shelf position 4/5. Select the Air Fry setting. Set the cooking temperature to 350°F/176°C and the cooking time to 8 minutes. Shake two times during cooking. They will feel soft initially but get crunchy as they cool. 3. Line a large baking sheet with parchment paper. 4. Place chocolate in a medium microwave-safe bowl. Microwave on high, heating in 20-second increments and stirring until melted. Place 1 teaspoon chocolate in a rounded mound on ungreased parchment-lined baking sheet, then press 1 pecan into top, repeating with remaining chocolate and pecans. 5. Place baking sheet into refrigerator to cool at least 30 minutes. Once cooled, store clusters in a large sealed container in refrigerator up to 5 days.

Flavorful Pumpkin Cookie with Cream Cheese Frosting

Prep Time: 10 minutes | Cook Time: 7 minutes | Serves: 6

½ cup blanched finely ground almond flour	½ teaspoon vanilla extract
½ cup powdered erythritol, divided	½ teaspoon pumpkin pie spice
2 tablespoons butter, softened	2 tablespoons pure pumpkin purée
1 large egg	½ teaspoon ground cinnamon, divided
½ teaspoon unflavored gelatin	¼ cup low-carb, sugar-free chocolate chips
½ teaspoon baking powder	3 ounces full-fat cream cheese, softened

1. In a large bowl, combine almond flour and ¼ cup erythritol. Stir in butter, egg, and gelatin until combined. 2. Stir in baking powder, vanilla, pumpkin purée, pumpkin pie spice, and ¼ teaspoon cinnamon, then fold in chocolate chips. 3. Pour batter into 6" round baking pan that fits in the appliance. 4. Slide the Wire Rack into shelf position 6 and place the pan on the Wire Rack. Select the Bake setting. Set the cooking temperature to 300°F/148°C and the cooking time to 7 minutes. 5. When fully cooked, the top will be golden brown and a toothpick inserted in center will come out clean. Let cool at least 20 minutes. 6. Make the frosting by mixing cream cheese, remaining ¼ teaspoon cinnamon, and remaining ¼ cup erythritol in a large bowl. Use an electric mixer to beat until it becomes fluffy. Spread onto the cooled cookie. Garnish with additional cinnamon if desired.

Basic Olive Oil Cake

Prep Time: 10 minutes | Cook Time: 30 minutes | Serves: 8

2 cups blanched finely ground almond flour
5 large eggs, whisked
¾ cup extra-virgin olive oil

⅓ cup granular erythritol
1 teaspoon vanilla extract
1 teaspoon baking powder

1. In a large bowl, mix up all ingredients. Pour batter into an ungreased 6" round nonstick baking dish that fits in the appliance. 2. Slide the Wire Rack into shelf position 6 and place the dish on the Wire Rack. Select the Bake setting. Set the cooking temperature to 300°F/148°C and the cooking time to 30 minutes. 3. The cake will be golden on top and firm in the center when done. 4. Let cake cool in dish 30 minutes before slicing and serving.

Low-Carb Chocolate-Covered Maple Bacon

Prep Time: 5 minutes | Cook Time: 12 minutes | Serves: 2

8 slices sugar-free bacon
1 tablespoon granular erythritol
⅓ cup low-carb, sugar-free chocolate chips

1 teaspoon coconut oil
½ teaspoon maple extract

1 Place bacon on the Baking Pan and sprinkle with erythritol. 2. Slide the Baking Pan into shelf position 4/5. 3. Select the Bacon setting. Set the cooking temperature to 350°F/176°C and the cooking time to 12 minutes. 4. Turn bacon halfway through the cooking time. Cook to desired doneness, checking at 9 minutes. 5. When bacon is done, set aside to cool. 6. In a small microwave-safe bowl, place chocolate chips and coconut oil. Microwave for 30 seconds and stir. Add in maple extract. 7. Place bacon onto a sheet of parchment. Drizzle chocolate over bacon and place in refrigerator to cool and harden, about 5 minutes.

Flavorful Brownies for Two

Prep Time: 5 minutes | Cook Time: 15 minutes | Serves: 2

½ cup blanched finely ground almond flour
3 tablespoons granular erythritol
3 tablespoons unsweetened cocoa powder
½ teaspoon baking powder

1 teaspoon vanilla extract
2 large eggs, whisked
2 tablespoons salted butter, melted

1. In a medium bowl, combine flour, erythritol, cocoa powder, and baking powder. 2. Add in vanilla, eggs, and butter, and stir until a thick batter forms. 3. Pour batter into two 4" ramekins greased with cooking spray and place ramekins on the Crisper Tray. Slide the Crisper Tray into shelf position 4/5. Select the Air Fry setting. Set the cooking temperature to 325°F/163°C and the cooking time to 15 minutes. 4. Centers will be firm when done. Let ramekins cool 5 minutes before serving.

Crispy Cinnamon Pretzels

Prep Time: 10 minutes | Cook Time: 10 minutes | Serves: 6

1½ cups shredded mozzarella cheese
1 cup blanched finely ground almond flour
2 tablespoons salted butter, melted, divided

¼ cup granular erythritol, divided
1 teaspoon ground cinnamon

1. Place mozzarella, flour, 1 tablespoon butter, and 2 tablespoons erythritol in a large microwave-safe bowl. Microwave on high for 45 seconds and whisk with a fork until a smooth dough ball forms. 2. Separate dough into six equal sections. Gently roll each section into a 12" rope and then fold into a pretzel shape. 3. Place pretzels on the Crisper Tray and slide the Crisper Tray into shelf position 4/5. Select the Air Fry setting. Set the cooking temperature to 370°F/187°C and the cooking time to 8 minutes. Turn the pretzels halfway through cooking. 4. In a small bowl, combine remaining butter, remaining erythritol, and cinnamon. Brush ½ mixture on both sides of pretzels. 5. Place pretzels back into the appliance and cook at 370°F/187°C for an additional 2 minutes. 6. Transfer pretzels to a large plate. Brush on both sides with remaining butter mixture, then let cool 5 minutes before serving.

Simple Keto Danish

Prep Time: 10 minutes | Cook Time: 12 minutes | Serves: 6

1½ cups shredded mozzarella cheese
½ cup blanched finely ground almond flour
3 ounces cream cheese, divided

¼ cup confectioners' erythritol
1 tablespoon lemon juice

1. Place mozzarella, flour, and 1 ounce cream cheese in a large microwave-safe bowl. Microwave on high for 45 seconds and whisk with a fork until a soft dough forms. 2. Separate dough into six equal sections and press each in a single layer into an ungreased 4" × 4" square nonstick baking dish that fits in the appliance to form six even squares that touch. 3. In a small bowl, mix remaining cream cheese, erythritol, and lemon juice. Place 1 tablespoon mixture in center of each piece of dough in baking dish. Fold all four corners of each dough piece halfway to center to reach cream cheese mixture. 4. Slide the Wire Rack into shelf position 6 and place the dish on the Wire Rack. Select the Bake setting. Set the cooking temperature to 320°F/160°C and the cooking time to 12 minutes. 5. The center and edges will be browned when done. Let cool 10 minutes before serving.

Fluffy Coconut Flour Cake

Prep Time: 10 minutes | Cook Time: 25 minutes | Serves: 6

2 tablespoons salted butter, melted
⅓ cup coconut flour
2 large eggs, whisked
½ cup granular erythritol

1 teaspoon baking powder
1 teaspoon vanilla extract
½ cup sour cream

1. Mix up all ingredients in a large bowl. Pour batter into an ungreased 6" round nonstick baking dish that fits in the appliance. 2. Slide the Wire Rack into shelf position 6 and place the dish on the Wire Rack. Select the Bake setting. Set the cooking temperature to 300°F/148°C and the cooking time to 25 minutes. 3. The cake will be dark golden on top, and a toothpick inserted in the center should come out clean when done. 4. Let cool in dish 15 minutes before slicing and serving.

Fresh Strawberry Shortcake

Prep Time: 10 minutes | Cook Time: 25 minutes | Serves: 6

2 tablespoons coconut oil
1 cup blanched finely ground almond flour
2 large eggs, whisked
½ cup granular erythritol

1 teaspoon baking powder
1 teaspoon vanilla extract
2 cups sugar-free whipped cream
6 medium fresh strawberries, hulled and sliced

1. In a large bowl, combine the coconut oil, flour, erythritol, baking powder, eggs, and vanilla. Pour batter into an ungreased 6" round nonstick baking dish that fits in the appliance. 2. Slide the Wire Rack into shelf position 6 and place the dish on the Wire Rack. Select the Bake setting. Set the cooking temperature to 300°F/148°C and the cooking time to 25 minutes. 3. When done, shortcake should be golden and a toothpick inserted in the middle will come out clean. 4. Remove dish and let cool 1 hour. 5. Once cooled, top cake with whipped cream and strawberries to serve.

Crispy Cinnamon Pork Rinds

Prep Time: 5 minutes | Cook Time: 5 minutes | Serves: 2

2 ounces pork rinds
2 tablespoons unsalted butter, melted

½ teaspoon ground cinnamon
¼ cup powdered erythritol

1. In a large bowl, toss pork rinds and butter. Sprinkle with cinnamon and erythritol and then toss to evenly coat. 2. Place pork rinds on the Baking Pan and slide the Baking Pan into shelf position 4/5. 3. Select the Air Fry setting. Set the cooking temperature to 400°F/204°C and the cooking time to 5 minutes. 4. When cooking is done, serve immediately.

Crispy Cream Cheese Shortbread Cookies

Prep Time: 40 minutes | Cook Time: 20 minutes | Serves: 6

¼ cup coconut oil, melted	1 large egg, whisked
2 ounces cream cheese, softened	2 cups blanched finely ground almond flour
½ cup granular erythritol	1 teaspoon almond extract

1. Mix up all ingredients in a large bowl to form a firm ball. 2. Place dough on a sheet of plastic wrap and roll into a 12"-long log shape. Roll log in plastic wrap and place in refrigerator 30 minutes to chill. 3. Remove log from plastic and slice into twelve equal cookies. Slice two sheets of parchment paper to fit the Crisper Tray. Place six cookies on each ungreased sheet. Place one sheet with cookies on the Crisper Tray and slide the Crisper Tray into shelf position 4/5. Select the Air Fry setting. Set the cooking temperature to 320°F/160°C and the cooking time to 10 minutes. Turn the cookies halfway through cooking. They will be lightly golden when done. Repeat with remaining cookies. 4. Let cool 15 minutes before serving to avoid crumbling.

Mini Flourless Chocolate Cakes

Prep Time: 10 minutes | Cook Time: 10 minutes | Serves: 8

Cake:	
½ cup (1 stick) unsalted butter (or coconut oil for dairy-free)	of powdered sweetener
4 ounces unsweetened chocolate, chopped	3 large eggs
¾ cup Swerve confectioners'-style sweetener or equivalent amount	
Filling:	
1 (8-ounce) package cream cheese (or Kite Hill brand cream cheese style spread for dairy-free), softened	¼ cup Swerve confectioners'-style sweetener or equivalent amount of powdered or liquid sweetener
For Garnish (Optional):	
Whipped cream	Raspberries

Make the cream filling: 1. In a medium-sized bowl, mix together the cream cheese and sweetener until well combined. Taste and add more sweetener if desired.
Make the cake batter: 1. Grease eight 4-ounce ramekins that fits in the appliance. 2. Heat the chocolate and butter in a saucepan over low heat, stirring often, until the chocolate is completely melted. Remove from the heat. 3. Add the sweetener and eggs and use a hand mixer on low to combine well. Set aside. 4. Divide the chocolate mixture among the greased ramekins, filling each one halfway. Place 1 tablespoon of the filling on top of the chocolate mixture in each ramekin. 5. Slide the Wire Rack into shelf position 6 and place the ramekins on the Wire Rack. Select the Bake setting. Set the cooking temperature to 375°F/190°C and the cooking time to 10 minutes. Cook until the outside is set and the inside is soft and warm. Let cool completely, top with whipped cream, if desired, and garnish with raspberries, if desired. 6. Store without whipped cream in an airtight container in the refrigerator for up to 4 days or in the freezer for up to a month. Serve leftovers chilled or reheat in the Air Fryer at 350°F/176°C for 5 minutes, or until heated through.

Tasty Mini Cheesecake

Prep Time: 10 minutes | Cook Time: 15 minutes | Serves: 2

½ cup walnuts	1 large egg
2 tablespoons salted butter	½ teaspoon vanilla extract
2 tablespoons granular erythritol	⅛ cup powdered erythritol
4 ounces full-fat cream cheese, softened	

1. Place walnuts, butter, and granular erythritol in a food processor. Pulse until ingredients stick together and a dough forms. 2. Press dough into 4" springform pan that fits in the appliance. Slide the Wire Rack into shelf position 6 and place the pan on the Wire Rack. 3. Select the Bake setting. Set the cooking temperature to 400°F/204°C and the cooking time to 5 minutes. 4. When the cooking is done, remove the crust and let cool. 5. In a medium bowl, mix together cream cheese with egg, vanilla extract, and powdered erythritol until smooth. 6. Spoon mixture on top of baked walnut crust and place into the appliance. 7. Cook at 300°F/148°C for 10 minutes. 8. Once done, chill for 2 hours before serving.

Yummy Pumpkin Cake

Prep Time: 10 minutes | Cook Time: 25 minutes | Serves: 8

4 tablespoons salted butter, melted
½ cup granular brown erythritol
¼ cup pure pumpkin puree
1 cup blanched finely ground almond flour

½ teaspoon baking powder
⅛ teaspoon salt
1 teaspoon pumpkin pie spice

1. Mix up all ingredients in a large bowl. Pour batter into an ungreased 6" round nonstick baking dish that fits in the appliance.
2. Slide the Wire Rack into shelf position 6 and place the dish on the Wire Rack. Select the Bake setting. Set the cooking temperature to 300°F/148°C and the cooking time to 25 minutes. 3. The top will be dark brown, and a toothpick inserted in the center should come out clean when done. Let cool 30 minutes before serving.

Lemony Blackberry Crisp

Prep Time: 5 minutes | Cook Time: 15 minutes | Serves: 4

2 cups blackberries
⅓ cup powdered erythritol
2 tablespoons lemon juice

¼ teaspoon xanthan gum
1 cup Crunchy Granola

1. In a large bowl, toss blackberries, erythritol, lemon juice, and xanthan gum. 2. Pour into 6" round baking dish that fits in the appliance and cover with foil. Slide the Wire Rack into shelf position 6 and place the dish on the Wire Rack. 3. Select the Bake setting. Set the cooking temperature to 350°F/176°C and the cooking time to 12 minutes. 4. When the cooking is complete, remove the foil and stir. 5. Sprinkle granola over mixture and return to the appliance. 6. Cook at 320°F/160°C for 3 minutes or until top is golden. 7. When cooking is complete, serve warm.

Homemade Chocolate Doughnut Holes

Prep Time: 10 minutes | Cook Time: 6 minutes | Serves: 10

1 cup blanched finely ground almond flour
½ cup low-carb vanilla protein powder
½ cup granular erythritol
¼ cup unsweetened cocoa powder

½ teaspoon baking powder
2 large eggs, whisked
½ teaspoon vanilla extract

1. Mix up all ingredients in a large bowl until a soft dough forms. Separate and roll dough into twenty balls, about 2 tablespoons each. 2. Cut a piece of parchment to the Crisper Tray. Working in batches if needed, place doughnut holes on the Crisper Tray on ungreased parchment. Slide Crisper Tray the into shelf position 4/5. Select the Air Fry setting. Set the cooking temperature to 380°F/193°C and the cooking time to 6 minutes. Then flip doughnut holes halfway through cooking. 3. Doughnut holes will be golden and firm when done. Let cool completely before serving, about 10 minutes.

Refreshing Lime Bars

Prep Time: 10 minutes | Cook Time: 33 minutes | Serves: 8

1½ cups blanched finely ground almond flour, divided
¾ cup confectioners' erythritol, divided
4 tablespoons salted butter, melted

½ cup fresh lime juice
2 large eggs, whisked

1. In a medium bowl, combine 1 cup flour, ¼ cup erythritol, and butter. Press mixture into bottom of an ungreased 6" round nonstick cake pan that fits in the appliance. 2. Slide the Wire Rack into shelf position 6 and place the pan on the Wire Rack. Select the Bake setting. Set the cooking temperature to 300°F/148°C and the cooking time to 13 minutes. 3. Crust will be brown and set in the middle when done. Allow to cool in pan 10 minutes. 4. In a medium bowl, combine remaining flour, lime juice, remaining erythritol, and eggs. Add mixture over cooled crust and return to the appliance to cook for 20 minutes 300°F/148°C. Top will be browned and firm when done. 5. Let cool completely in pan for about 30 minutes and then chill covered in the refrigerator 1 hour. Serve chilled.

Yummy Halle Berries–and–Cream Cobbler

Prep Time: 10 minutes | Cook Time: 25 minutes | Serves: 4

12 ounces cream cheese (1½ cups), softened
1 large egg
¾ cup Swerve confectioners'-style sweetener or equivalent amount of powdered sweetener
Biscuits:
3 large egg whites
¾ cup blanched almond flour
1 teaspoon baking powder
Frosting:
2 ounces cream cheese (¼ cup), softened
1 tablespoon Swerve confectioners'-style sweetener or equivalent amount of powdered or liquid sweetener

½ teaspoon vanilla extract
¼ teaspoon fine sea salt
1 cup sliced fresh raspberries or strawberries

2½ tablespoons very cold unsalted butter, cut into pieces (see Tip)
¼ teaspoon fine sea salt

1 tablespoon unsweetened, unflavored almond milk or heavy cream
Fresh raspberries or strawberries, for garnish

1. Grease a 7-inch pie pan that fits in the appliance. 2. In a large mixing bowl, combine the egg, cream cheese, and sweetener with a hand mixer and mix until smooth. Stir in the vanilla and salt and gently fold in the raspberries with a rubber spatula. Add the mixture to the prepared pan and set aside. 3. Make the biscuits by placing the egg whites in a medium-sized mixing bowl. Using a hand mixer, whip the egg whites until very fluffy and stiff. Alternatively, you can use the bowl of a stand mixer to whip the egg whites. 4. In a separate medium-sized bowl, combine the baking powder and almond flour. Cut in the butter and add the salt, stirring gently to keep the butter pieces intact. 5. Gently fold the almond flour mixture into the egg whites. Using a large spoon or ice cream scooper, scoop out the dough and form it into a 2-inch-wide biscuit, ensuring the butter stays in separate clumps. Place the biscuit over the raspberry mixture in the pan. Repeat with the remaining dough to make 4 biscuits. 6. Slide the Wire Rack into shelf position 6 and place the pan on the Wire Rack. Select the Bake setting. Set the cooking temperature to 400°F/204°C and the cooking time to 5 minutes. Then reduce the temperature to 325°F/163°C and bake for another 17 to 20 minutes, until the biscuits are golden brown. 7. While the cobbler cooks, make the frosting by placing the cream cheese in a small bowl and stir to break it up. Stir in the sweetener and then stir in the almond milk until well combined. If you like a thinner frosting, add more almond milk. 8. Remove the cobbler and allow to cool slightly, then drizzle with the frosting. Garnish with fresh raspberries. 9. Store leftovers in an airtight container in the refrigerator for up to 3 days. Reheat the cobbler in the Air Fryer at 350°F/176°C for 3 minutes, or until warmed through.

Almond Butter Chocolate Chip Balls

Prep Time: 5 minutes | Cook Time: 10 minutes | Serves: 10

1 cup almond butter
1 large egg
1 teaspoon vanilla extract
¼ cup low-carb protein powder

¼ cup powdered erythritol
¼ cup shredded unsweetened coconut
¼ cup low-carb, sugar-free chocolate chips
½ teaspoon ground cinnamon

1. In a large bowl, mix almond butter and egg. Add in vanilla, protein powder, and erythritol. 2. Fold in coconut, chocolate chips, and cinnamon. Roll into 1" balls. Place balls on the Baking Pan and slide the Baking Pan into shelf position 4/5. 3. Select the Air Fry setting. Set the cooking temperature to 320°F/160°C and the cooking time to 10 minutes. 4. Allow to cool completely. Store in an airtight container in the refrigerator up to 4 days.

Pecan and Chocolate Chip Brownies

Prep Time: 10 minutes | Cook Time: 20 minutes | Serves: 6

½ cup blanched finely ground almond flour
½ cup powdered erythritol
2 tablespoons unsweetened cocoa powder
½ teaspoon baking powder

¼ cup unsalted butter, softened
1 large egg
¼ cup chopped pecans
¼ cup low-carb, sugar-free chocolate chips

1. In a large bowl, mix up almond flour, cocoa powder, erythritol, and baking powder. Stir in butter and egg. 2. Fold in pecans and chocolate chips. Scoop mixture into 6" round baking pan that fits in the appliance. Slide the Wire Rack into shelf position 6 and place the pan on the Wire Rack. 3. Select the Bake setting. Set the cooking temperature to 300°F/148°C and the cooking time to 20 minutes. 4. When fully cooked a toothpick inserted in center will come out clean. Allow 20 minutes to fully cool and firm up.

Mini Chocolate Espresso Cheesecake

Prep Time: 5 minutes | Cook Time: 15 minutes | Serves: 2

½ cup walnuts
2 tablespoons salted butter
2 tablespoons granular erythritol
4 ounces full-fat cream cheese, softened
1 large egg

½ teaspoon vanilla extract
2 tablespoons powdered erythritol
2 teaspoons unsweetened cocoa powder
1 teaspoon espresso powder

1. Place walnuts, butter, and granular erythritol in a food processor. Pulse until ingredients stick together and a dough forms. 2. Press dough into 4" springform pan that fits in the appliance. Slide the Wire Rack into shelf position 6 and place the pan on the Wire Rack. 3. Select the Bake setting. Set the cooking temperature to 400°F/204°C and the cooking time to 5 minutes. 4. When cooking is done, remove crust and let cool. 5. In a medium bowl, mix together cream cheese, egg, powdered erythritol, cocoa powder, vanilla extract, and espresso powder until smooth. 6. Spoon mixture on top of baked walnut crust and place into the appliance. 7. Cook at 300°F/148°C for 10 minutes. 8. Once done, chill for 2 hours before serving.

Fluffy Little French Fudge Cakes

Prep Time: 10 minutes | Cook Time: 25 minutes | Serves: 12

Cakes:

3 cups blanched almond flour
¾ cup unsweetened cocoa powder
1 teaspoon baking soda
½ teaspoon fine sea salt
6 large eggs
1 cup Swerve confectioners'-style sweetener or equivalent amount of powdered sweetener

1½ cups canned pumpkin puree
3 tablespoons brewed decaf espresso or other strong brewed decaf coffee
3 tablespoons unsalted butter, melted but not hot (or coconut oil for dairy-free)
1 teaspoon vanilla extract

Cream Cheese Frosting:

½ cup Swerve confectioners'-style sweetener or equivalent amount of powdered or liquid sweetener
½ cup (1 stick) unsalted butter, melted (or coconut oil for dairy-free)

4 ounces cream cheese (½ cup) (or Kite Hill brand cream cheese style spread for dairy-free), softened
3 tablespoons unsweetened, unflavored almond milk or heavy cream

Chocolate Drizzle:

3 tablespoons unsalted butter, melted (or coconut oil for dairy-free)
2 tablespoons Swerve confectioners'-style sweetener or equivalent amount of powdered or liquid sweetener

2 tablespoons unsweetened cocoa powder
¼ cup unsweetened, unflavored almond milk
½ cup chopped walnuts or pecans, for garnish (optional)

Make the frosting: 1. In a large bowl, mix the sweetener, melted butter, and cream cheese until well combined. Add the almond milk and stir well to combine.

Make the chocolate drizzle: 1. In a small bowl, stir together the melted butter, sweetener, and cocoa powder until well combined. Add the almond milk while stirring to thin the mixture.

Make the cakes: 1. Spray 2 mini Bundt pans that fits in the appliance with coconut oil. 2. In a medium-sized bowl, whisk together the flour, baking soda, cocoa powder, and salt until blended. 3. In a large bowl, use a hand mixer to beat the eggs and sweetener until light and fluffy, 2 to 3 minutes. Add the pumpkin puree, espresso, melted butter, and vanilla and stir to combine. 4. Pour the wet ingredients into the dry ingredients and stir until just combined. 5. Add the batter to the prepared pans, filling each well two-thirds full. Slide the Wire Rack into shelf position 6 and place the pan on the Wire Rack, working in batches. Select the Bake setting. Set the cooking temperature to 350°F/176°C and the cooking time to 25 minutes. Cook for 20 to 25 minutes until a toothpick inserted into the center of a cake comes out clean. 6. Let the cakes cool completely in the pans before removing them. 7. After the cakes have cooled, dip the tops of the cakes into the frosting, then use a spoon to drizzle the chocolate over each frosted cake. Garnish the cakes with chopped nuts, if desired. 8. Store leftovers in an airtight container in the refrigerator for up to 4 days or in the freezer for up to a month.

Crispy Pecan Snowball Cookies

Prep Time: 5 minutes | Cook Time: 24 minutes | Serves: 6

1 cup chopped pecans
½ cup salted butter, melted
½ cup coconut flour

¾ cup confectioners' erythritol, divided
1 teaspoon vanilla extract

1. In a food processor, blend together pecans, flour, ½ cup erythritol, butter, and vanilla 1 minute until a dough forms. 2. Form dough into twelve individual cookie balls, about 1 tablespoon each. 3. Cut three pieces of parchment to the Crisper Tray. Place four cookies on each ungreased parchment and place a piece of parchment with cookies on the Crisper Tray. Slide the Crisper Tray into shelf position 4/5. Select the Air Fry setting. Set the cooking temperature to 325°F/163°C and the cooking time to 8 minutes. Repeat cooking with remaining batches. 4. When the cooking is complete, allow cookies to cool 5 minutes on a large serving plate until cool enough to handle. While still warm, dust cookies with remaining erythritol. Let cool completely for about 15 minutes, before serving.

Chocolate Chip Pan Cookie

Prep Time: 10 minutes | Cook Time: 7 minutes | Serves: 4

½ cup blanched finely ground almond flour
¼ cup powdered erythritol
2 tablespoons unsalted butter, softened
1 large egg

½ teaspoon unflavored gelatin
½ teaspoon baking powder
½ teaspoon vanilla extract
2 tablespoons low-carb, sugar-free chocolate chips

1. In a large bowl, mix up almond flour and erythritol. Stir in butter, egg, and gelatin until combined. 2. Stir in baking powder and vanilla and then fold in chocolate chips. Pour batter into 6" round baking pan that fits in the appliance. Slide the Wire Rack into shelf position 6 and place the pan on the Wire Rack. 3. Select the Bake setting. Set the cooking temperature to 300°F/148°C and the cooking time to 7 minutes. 4. When fully cooked, the top will be golden brown and a toothpick inserted in center will come out clean. Let cool at least 10 minutes.

Mini Peanut Butter Cheesecake

Prep Time: 10 minutes | Cook Time: 10 minutes | Serves: 2

4 ounces cream cheese, softened
2 tablespoons confectioners' erythritol
1 tablespoon all-natural, no-sugar-added peanut butter

½ teaspoon vanilla extract
1 large egg, whisked

1. In a medium bowl, combine cream cheese and erythritol until smooth. Mix in peanut butter and vanilla until smooth. Add egg and stir just until combined. 2. Spoon mixture into an ungreased 4" springform nonstick pan that fits in the appliance. Slide the Wire Rack into shelf position 6 and place the pan on the Wire Rack. Select the Bake setting. Set the cooking temperature to 300°F/148°C and the cooking time to 10 minutes. Edges will be firm, but center will be mostly set with only a small amount of jiggle when done. 3. Let pan cool at room temperature 30 minutes, cover with plastic wrap, then place into refrigerator at least 2 hours. Serve chilled.

Conclusion

This Emeril Lagasse French Door air fryer cookbook is a culinary gem! Its comprehensive collection of recipes, accompanied by clear instructions and helpful tips, has truly revolutionized my cooking experience. The diverse range of dishes allows me to explore new flavors and cuisines, all while utilizing the incredible features of my air fryer. The cookbook's emphasis on healthy cooking techniques, such as air frying with minimal oil, has empowered me to make better dietary choices without compromising on taste. This appliance has many features. Furthermore, the inclusion of suggested accessories and cooking times for optimal results has been immensely helpful in achieving restaurant-quality dishes from the comfort of my own kitchen. Overall, this cookbook has exceeded my expectations and has become an indispensable resource in my culinary journey. I highly recommend it to anyone looking to unlock the full potential of their air fryer.

Appendix 1 Measurement Conversion Chart

WEIGHT EQUIVALENTS

US STANDARD	METRIC (APPROXIMATE)
1 ounce	28 g
2 ounces	57 g
5 ounces	142 g
10 ounces	284 g
15 ounces	425 g
16 ounces (1 pound)	455 g
1.5pounds	680 g
2pounds	907 g

VOLUME EQUIVALENTS (LIQUID)

US STANDARD	US STANDARD (OUNCES)	METRIC (APPROXIMATE)
2 tablespoons	1 fl.oz	30 mL
¼ cup	2 fl.oz	60 mL
½ cup	4 fl.oz	120 mL
1 cup	8 fl.oz	240 mL
1½ cup	12 fl.oz	355 mL
2 cups or 1 pint	16 fl.oz	475 mL
4 cups or 1 quart	32 fl.oz	1 L
1 gallon	128 fl.oz	4 L

VOLUME EQUIVALENTS (DRY)

US STANDARD	METRIC (APPROXIMATE)
⅛ teaspoon	0.5 mL
¼ teaspoon	1 mL
½ teaspoon	2 mL
¾ teaspoon	4 mL
1 teaspoon	5 mL
1 tablespoon	15 mL
¼ cup	59 mL
½ cup	118 mL
¾ cup	177 mL
1 cup	235 mL
2 cups	475 mL
3 cups	700 mL
4 cups	1 L

TEMPERATURES EQUIVALENTS

FAHRENHEIT(F)	CELSIUS(C) (APPROXIMATE)
225 °F	107 °C
250 °F	120 °C
275 °F	135 °C
300 °F	150 °C
325 °F	160 °C
350 °F	180 °C
375 °F	190 °C
400 °F	205 °C
425 °F	220 °C
450 °F	235 °C
475 °F	245 °C
500 °F	260 °C

Appendix 2 Air Fryer Cooking Chart

Frozen Foods	Temp (°F)	Time (min)
Onion Rings (12 oz.)	400	8
Thin French Fries (20 oz.)	400	14
Thick French Fries (17 oz.)	400	18
Pot Sticks (10 oz.)	400	8
Fish Sticks (10 oz.)	400	10
Fish Fillets (½-inch, 10 oz.)	400	14

vegetables	Temp (°F)	Time (min)
Asparagus (1-inch slices)	400	5
Beets (sliced)	350	25
Beets (whole)	400	40
Bell Peppers (sliced)	350	13
Broccoli	400	6
Brussels Sprouts (halved)	380	15
Carrots(½-inch slices)	380	15
Cauliflower (florets)	400	12
Eggplant (1½-inch cubes)	400	15
Fennel (quartered)	370	15
Mushrooms (¼-inch slices)	400	5
Onion (pearl)	400	10
Parsnips (½-inch chunks)	380	5
Peppers (1-inch chunks)	400	15
Potatoes (baked, whole)	400	40
Squash (½-inch chunks)	400	12
Tomatoes (cherry)	400	4
Zucchni (½-inch sticks)	400	12

Meat	Temp (°F)	Time (min)
Bacon	400	5 to 7
Beef Eye Round Roast (4 lbs.)	390	50 to 60
Burger (4 oz.)	370	16 to 20
Chicken Breasts, bone-in (1.25 lbs.)	370	25
Chicken Breasts, boneless (4 oz.)	380	12
Chicken Drumsticks (2.5 lbs.)	370	20
Chicken Thighs, bone-in (2 lbs.)	380	22
Chicken Thighs, boneless (1.5 lbs.)	380	18 to 20
Chicken Legs, bone-in (1.75 lbs.)	380	30
Chicken Wings (2 lbs.)	400	12
Flank Steak (1.5 lbs.)	400	12
Game Hen (halved, 2 lbs.)	390	20
Loin (2 lbs.)	360	55
London Broil (2 lbs.)	400	20 to 28
Meatballs (3-inch)	380	10
Rack of Lamb (1.5-2 lbs.)	380	22
Sausages	380	15
Whole Chicken (6.5 lbs.)	360	75

Fish and Seafood	Temp (°F)	Time (min)
Calamari (8 oz.)	400	4
Fish Fillet (1-inch, 8 oz.)	400	10
Salmon Fillet (6 oz.)	380	12
Tuna Steak	400	7 to 10
Scallops	400	5 to 7
Shrimp	400	5

Appendix 3 Recipes Index

Made in the USA
Las Vegas, NV
24 November 2024

12567437R00065